I dedicate this book to every person who is opening it with curiosity and enthusiasm, who has dreams to live a life of meaning and contribution.

And I dedicate this book to my father, Steve Swanepoel, who has been my inspiration to be the best version of myself daily, and who taught me the value of relationships and the power of giving.

I also want to dedicate this book to all the men and women throughout the years who had the will and selflessness to share their life-changing wisdom, through books, programmes and talks, with those eager for a new path. I did my best to soak in all that I read, heard and observed, and in turn, what I learnt seeped into my thoughts and my words and my deeds, and some of these core principles have become part of my teaching and sharing with others, paying it forward. What you read in these pages are my real-life experiences, through my successes and failures, and processes that I developed through trial and error over time, which I have applied successfully in my own life, and that I have also shared with thousands of other individuals that have also received tremendous value from implementing it into their own lives. But they have been greatly enriched by all the others who have walked the path before me, and for that I am very grateful.

This dedication, then, is my way of recognising all the people who have made such a big difference in my life. I am hoping that in the same way, I will serve you, and this book will make an equally big difference in your life.

Table of Contents

Foreword ix
Acknowledgements xi

Chapter 1 – How My Connected Story Began. 1
The Power of the Spirit of Ubuntu 1
What's in a Name? 3
The Large Whiskey Bottle 5
A Destiny Announced at Birth. 7
The Bridge Builder Serving Humanity 10
The Global Citizen 13

Chapter 2 – Why Tell the Story Now? 15
Standing on the Backs of Giants. 15
COVID Shook Me to Action. 17
Who Has My Back? 19
Good Idea, Good Partner; What Is More Important?. 21
Why Is the Timing Now for You? 22
The "Haves" and the "Have Nots" 24

Chapter 3 – Why Do You Want to Be Connected? 27
Don't Take Only My Word for It 27
Are You Crushing It in Business, and Being Crushed at Home?. . . . 29
Lessons from the African Village 32
The Hungry Street Man. 34
Are You Careful, Careless or Caring? 36
Have Everything in Life You Want. 38

Chapter 4 – The Average of 5 41
If You Wanna Get Sick, Hang Out with Sick People 41
By Design, or Consequential 43
The Wisdom of the Ancient Greeks 46
The Simple Maths of Connections 48
The Train to Collective Genius 50
The Two-Stick Dance, Quality and Quantity 52

Chapter 5 – Quality, Quantity or Both? 55
Understanding My Relationship Mix 55
The Art of Relationships 58
What Does Your Vesica Piscis Tell You? 59
The Power of a Greeting 62
The Shelf Packer Named Philemon 65
5 Steps to Building My Relationship Currency 67

Chapter 6 – Getting Started on My Connected Journey 71
The Origin of Connector Currency – The Reptilian Brain 71
The Himba Poacher 74
Clash of the Cultures 77
Creating My Connector Mindset – My Inner Process 81
Creating My Connector Mindset – My Outer Process 83
The Big Five, the Little Five and the Micro Five 85

Chapter 7 – My Connector Strategy 89
River Rafting in Colorado 89
My Clarity Mapping Tool 92
Connector Strategy – The Big Who 94
Connector Strategy – The Big What 98
Connector Strategy – The Big Why 102
Seven Levels Deep 104

Chapter 8 – My Connector Action Map..................109
Retracing the Map..109
The Poor Kid from Pittsburgh............................111
Planning to Prosper..114
Taking Action..116
Why a Coach?..118
The Power of Connectivity...............................120

Chapter 9 – What to Keep in Mind When You Build It.........123
What Is the Magic Sauce?.................................123
How Many Faces Do You See?............................125
Code of the Extraordinary Mind..........................129
Is Relational Capital a Balance Sheet Entry?..................132
Social Media and Internet Have an Important Role to Play......134
The Lady with the Titanium Digital Rolodex..................137

Chapter 10 - How to Get the Best Return on Relational Capital (RORC)..141
Be Vulnerable...141
Be Ready 144
Be Relevant 146
Be Open to Listening.......................................149
Identify Your Dream Team 151
Cast a Big Shadow on Departure 154

Foreword

Are you in control of your own life, surrounded by the people who can help you to have the life you wish to live? Or does life feel hard and uncertain to you? Do you feel empty at times and wish to feel supported and connected with others instead?

No matter who you are or what your current situation is, regardless of your age, culture, beliefs, business or career, this book is full of insights and will act as a guide in your life, advising you on the steps to take to get clear on what the best direction is for you to take next, and who the right people are that can best support you in achieving your goals.

Ezanne Swanepoel has written *The Connected Rainmaker: Lead with Giving, and the Rest Will Come* so that you can turn your challenges and uncertainties into success, just as she did. After a heartbreaking, near-death experience, Ezanne decided to reset her life, and she immigrated from South Africa to Canada. She had to find her feet and her direction, and build relationships while being faced with the continuous challenges of COVID–being isolated in a new country, with change and uncertainty being the theme of the day. She is now the CEO of her company, The African Rainmaker Group, and she is a true example of what you can become when you apply everything she teaches you in this book.

In a very open and warm way, Ezanne welcomes you into her world, sharing with you many personal experiences to help you to overcome your fear of uncertainty and change, get clear on your direction, and

For bonuses go to www.connectedrainmaker.com

build the connections you need in order to live the impactful life you wish to live.

So, whether your dream is to lead a company, be a top producer in your field, overcome the self-destructive habits that hold you back, or make a difference in the larger world, you will need to recognize the true value and potential of building your connectedness, and how to expand this into a connected community. To build this valuable asset you will need a roadmap and a clear strategy on how to execute with deliberate and authentic intent. This book will take you through a 5-step process to help you gain clarity on the direction you wish to take, and who to take the journey with.

Get ready to read this amazing journey and get started on creating massive change in your life and finances, and tapping into your leadership currency.

Raymond Aaron
New York Times **Bestselling Author**

Acknowledgements

To write a book like this takes a lot of support and encouragement, and I want to thank all the amazing people who surround my life. Of course, to include everyone who has cheered on this effort would take too many pages, but I would like to thank a few.

I would like to thank **Daniel St Jacques** for pushing me to write this book. From watching him, I have learnt about the power of taking imperfect action. I am extremely grateful to him for all the support he has given me, and for his patience when I would spend hours staring at my screen and being in my own world.

I would like to thank my father, **Steve Swanepoel**, and my mother, **Liza Swanepoel,** for raising me to be the person I am today. I would not have been able to achieve all of my success if not for the endless love, guidance and patience that you have both given me. From watching my dad, I have learned the immense value of helping others, and from watching my mom, I have learnt to never give up and that you can achieve anything you want to achieve.

I appreciate the unconditional love that I have always received from my middle sister, **Celecia Stadler**, and her husband, **Jeanne Stadler**, and my gorgeous niece, **Jeleze**, and sweet nephew, **Ariel**. I have learnt from Celecia what it means to be truly selfless and give your everything to others, and from Jeanne I have learnt what it means to not sweat the small stuff, and from the two little ones I have learnt to laugh more; they always have the most beautiful smiles on their little faces.

For bonuses go to ...

I appreciate the unwavering and unconditional love that I have received from my baby sister, **Zanelle Dalglish**, and my brother-in-law, **Clint Dalglish**, and my handsome little nephew, **Tyler Dalglish**, and **Mrs. Trish Dalglish**. I have learnt from Zanellie how a beautiful woman with a huge heart, can be tough in a constructive way when the situation warrants it, and Clint has shown me that no matter how hard the road, he is someone that always stands by those he loves, through thick and thin. And my sweet Tyler, you have taught me the power of a heartfelt '"love you, bye" and bringing humour into any situation to make it lighter and better; you are just the cutest little thing. Mrs. D, you have taught me what it means to be selfless and loving.

I deeply appreciate the love, support and belief from all my family members, for attending my events, my award ceremonies, and also for being there for the celebrations that matter and supporting in the difficult moments. You have been part of my journey, understanding the value and the power of feeling like someone always has your back. To my grandfather, **Dr. Hennie Saayman** (one of my best friends), and my grandmother, **Lily Saayman**; my aunts and uncles, **Anso Le Grange, Linda and Johan Ferreira**, and **Riette and Robin Duncan**; to my cousins **Tian and Chane Fensham, Chane and Liaan Bosman, Stephan and Antoinette Ferreira**, and **John Ferreira**, my small cousins **Christian** and **Annebelle** and the extended family, a heartfelt thank you for being part of my life. The knowledge of having a loving support base has been instrumental to my confidence and perseverance to write my book.

Carmen St. Jacques (BM), thank you very much for your example of unconditional love; you have a capacity to love and to give in a way that few people ever master. I appreciate your belief and encouragement as I was writing my book.

Simon and Olivier St. Jacques, & Emily Beauchemin, your young adult spirits in my life in Canada have been a reminder and an inspiration for me to move forward with resilience and perseverance, even when the road did feel uphill at times, because when I look at you, I am reminded of the beautiful, talented young people that need support and guidance from our older generation to make their impact, and it makes me work harder to bring my contribution to the world, and to live up to being worthy of holding a torch for you.

Johanne Touchette, as a friend and a soul sister, your support and contribution in my life in the last few years has been so much more than words can express; a deep thank you and gratitude for the gift of your friendship. I am deeply in gratitude to you and **Andre Goyette.**

Diane Touchette, we are connected in a soulful way, beyond the confinement of expressed words. You have been my biggest support in birthing my book to reality. Thank you for putting your eyes on this book, guiding me forward and pushing me to think bigger by supporting my marketing and media efforts. I am deeply in gratitude to you and **Bryan Foye.**

Of course, I would like to acknowledge **ALL of my friends** for being such amazing people, for being my exquisite woven tapestry of connectedness. I am very blessed to have much more than two hands full of significant friendships around the world, people that REALLY have my back, from north to south, from east to west, and everywhere in between. The fact that I do not name each of you by name is not because you are not important to me; as I write my acknowledgements, I realise how blessed I am to have many really close and special friends in my life, and truthfully I would not want to miss any one of your names. I know that you know who you are, so please accept my gratitude, my appreciation and my love for you and your role in my life.

My **Henley Business School** family, we have grown together from your very humble beginnings, right to your moment of being awarded Best Business School in Africa. **Jon Foster-Pedley** and **Linda Buckley**, your collaborative approach to leadership, alongside all the other beautiful

For bonuses go to ...

individuals that I get to work, learn and grow with, is very difficult to match anywhere else. You truly build the leaders that build the businesses that build Africa. Thank you for the huge honour to continue being part of the Henley Oldies.

My **Kedge Business School** family, I have had the privilege to walk a 15-year-long path with you to date. You have become not only valued colleagues and students, but you are also friends. Thank you for providing such a solid platform where we can together make an impact in the business world, shaping the leaders of the present and the future. I feel blessed to be a part of you.

To **Raymond Aaron** and **10-10-10 Publishing,** thank you for helping me put together this book. Raymond, it does not require quantity of time to be deeply impacted by you. Thank you very much for all your support, guidance and encouragement, and for taking the time to respond so wisely and lovingly to my continuous enquiring mind; you so patiently listen and respond from the heart always. You are a fountain of wisdom, and I am a sponge that eagerly soaks it up. Not only do you continue to be a mentor to me, but you have also afforded me the privilege to call you a business partner. Everything about you is quality, and I am so grateful that I get to bathe in your wisdom frequently. I appreciate you.

To **Donna Karan** (DKNY), thank you for taking the time to share your experience and your heart with me, in Los Angeles in 2013. Your focus and heart-based mission to make Urban Zen a reality, inspired me to continue my work in Africa, to empower people in impoverished communities. I have continued to watch your progress as a businesswoman, and your spirit of collaboration with people like Kenneth Cole (Gentle Souls), to fulfil a meaningful and impactful mission, and it has given me hope when the road seems difficult.

Dean Graziosi, your energy and passion for business, your love for your wife and your children, and your love and drive for us, your KBB family, has been infectious. Thank you for all the doors you continue to open, and for the example you set for those that want to follow and contribute to something meaningful in life.

Tony Robbins, I know you are an icon to many. To me you were, and continue to be, a light that shows me direction when I really feel like I am in a dark place, or just directionless. Twice, in significant times in my life, I have turned to your guidance and your leadership to find my way back to fulfilling my mission. You have many attributes that I aspire to build as part of my own identity, and for all of these gifts that you bring into my life, I have deep gratitude and appreciation.

I deeply appreciate the wisdom you have offered me, **Keith Ferrazi**. I have received your coaching through virtual programmes, books, and Mindvalley. Your insights have helped me to realise what an important gift I have inside of me, and that it needs to be shared with the world.

Warren Buffet, a deep thank you for your solid and authentic example to me from a young age; you showed me that it is possible to care about people, be authentic to yourself and be principled, while building business success. You have been an inspiration to me, reminding me that it is possible to be all of this and succeed, when I saw many examples of the opposite behaviour around me at times through my career.

John Kasaona, the **Namibian Government** and **World Wildlife Fund**, I want to thank you for being an example of how through collaborative networks, we can bring together an integrated solution, a co-elevated community, that can serve the betterment of all people concerned, while preserving our beautiful nature and wildlife.

To my fellow **Africans and South Africans,** thank you for a lifetime of rich experiences that have moulded me into the woman I am today. Your spirit of Ubuntu, your warmth and kindness, goes with me wherever I am in the world. Many of my beautiful memories and

For bonuses go to ...

exemplary stories, which I have shared in my book, are thanks to our paths crossing over a lifetime of impactful moments.

To my fellow **Canadians,** thank you for welcoming me into this beautiful country and making me part of this nation. You brought me a sense of safety when I needed it, and offered me support and access to tremendous minds that have helped me extract my heart's message and put it into a book to share with the world.

Colin Hall and **Steve Hall,** you are both very dear to me, and I have learnt and shared so much with both of you. Thank you so much for all the opportunities you have created for me to grow, for the wisdom and philosophies that you have so generously shared with me. Some of the key principles in my book have been inspired by seeds that you planted in my mind and heart, and for this I truly thank you.

Donald Batal, thank you for sharing your creative mind with me, about how to share my message and my book with the world. You are always so generous with your time, ideas and resources. Having you as a sounding board at times while writing my book, has been much appreciated.

Richard Branson, many years ago, I had the opportunity to meet you in South Africa, although briefly. Through your books, practical examples and talks, your creative mind, supported by caring human-based principles, have continued to inspire me to reach higher and to impact more people. Thank you for being a shining example to me, to dream big and to reach wide to impact as many people as I can meaningfully.

Robin Sharma, your book, *The Monk Who Sold His Ferrari*, is a book that has elicited so many emotions, opportunities for growth, and has inspired me in so many meaningful ways to live a life of contribution, while striving to be my best version. At times in my life, this book was like a roadmap to me. I dream of a day when I can stand next to you on a stage and make a difference in people's lives collaboratively. I want to thank you for being a constant guide and teacher to me.

Peter Diamandis, you are an exemplary innovator, leader and entrepreneur. I had the opportunity to listen to you in person in Johannesburg, South Africa, a few years ago. I have dedicated almost my entire career to being an entrepreneur, which also has made me discover the untold secrets of the power of authentic relationships. I want to thank you for everything that I have learnt and continue to learn from you, through your books, videos and speeches, and through the work that you continue to do in Africa.

Dr. John Demartini, it has been such a privilege to have met you multiple times. Your mind is truly like no other person I have ever met. I share a great love for learning, consuming large quantities of information and translating that into meaningful nuggets of impactful information. I continue to listen to your DVDs, CDs, YouTube videos and live webinars, and I attend your programmes and read your books. Every time I have a touch point with your teachings, I grow more, and I get inspired to follow my mission of sharing my messages with others in the same way that you have impacted my life. Thank you so very much for being a guiding light to me.

Richard Rohr, you are a shining light that opens the minds, hearts and souls of people. You are a phenomenal catalyst that allows us to challenge our thinking and our behaviour, and you are so much more than that. I want to thank you for the profound wisdom you have shared with me over my life. I have meditated for days and months on some of your quotes, providing me with fertile ground to make profound breakthroughs in myself. Thank you very much for being an example to me as an author, and for being a spiritual guide in my life.

Ilze Alberts, it is such a joy to call you a close friend and to share a professional platform with you as a kindred spirit and partner in impacting the lives of others in a meaningful way. We have grown

For bonuses go to ...

together from strength to strength, and I thank you for your unconditional love, support and contributions as I have written this book.

Frans Van Der Colff, you echo the African Spirit of Ubuntu, in business, in friendship and in life. Thank you so much for the gift of having you as a business partner, and for the support you have given me, and the insights and stories you have shared as a support to me in completing my book.

Dr. William Danko, I respect you greatly as an author, and want to thank and acknowledge you for the depth of insight you have brought to me during my research for my book. You have such a deep understanding on the topic of wealth formation, and our discussions allowed me to crystallise some key concepts or secrets that the wealthy apply to relationships. Despite your busy schedule and being in such high demand, you always make a moment for me, and I appreciate this graciously.

Byron Tully, you are such a talented author, and you have such a wealth of knowledge, coupled with a generous heart and mind. I want to thank you for all the wisdom you have so graciously shared with me about how the "Old Money" people do things when it comes to relationships. I also want to acknowledge and thank you for the contribution you have made through our discussions, in my book.

Mark Timm, everything that you stand for in business, in family and in life is inspirational to me. Every time I have the opportunity to speak to you, I grow beyond measure. You have so selflessly given me so much wisdom, insight and guidance in a short period of time. I dream of a time where I can work alongside you, learning from you, and paying that wisdom forward to impact many other people globally. A heartfelt thank you for being so open to engage with me, guide me and share with me. Some of your wisdom has already been paid forward through the writing of this book.

Brett Will, you have a brilliant strategic mind, combined with the largest heart...this combination makes you a gift to this world. Your ability to turn any situation into a great business idea, while impacting many, is so inspirational to me; I always learn from you. Thank you for the many conversations we have had while I have written my book; you challenge my thinking and help me to stretch my mind, and I appreciate your very meaningful contribution.

Loral Langemeier, you really are the Millionaire Maker!! We met already 10 years ago—can you believe it—and since then, you have been a constant support, coach and guide for me in "millionaire mindset" and in the world of making money. For this, I deeply thank you, and also for your continued support as I completed this book; you believed in me and encouraged me to go for it. I actually did it; thank you!!

Jon and Missy Butcher, it has been a privilege to walk a 12-Category Smart Journey with you through Lifebook, and more recently as we have taken hands in business to share the gift of Lifebook with the world. You know that connections and relationships are very important to me, and you have been a shining example of what it means to get the relationship thing right as life partners, for you as husband and wife. I look forward to the possibility to continue our collaboration, maybe in a sequel book— *Connections – The Real Marriage Currency*. Thank you for the privilege to work with you, to grow with you and to learn from you.

Prof. Dr. Rasoava Rijamampianina (Rija), our journey started together with you as my MBA professor; since then, you have become a valued mentor, colleague and friend. You have such a passion for life, and you are the essence of what a teacher should be. Your approach to sharing and listening has a way of bringing out the best in me. Thank you for believing in me, thank you for your encouragement as I was writing my book, and thank you for the valuable contributions that you have made to my book through our conversations and storytelling.

For bonuses go to ...

Dr. Shadrick Mazaza, thank you for sharing your intricate knowledge of personal transformation. Your insights as a physician and philosopher of transformation and consciousness have been very impactful in informing parts of my book.

Terry Booysen, thank you for your generosity of time and knowledge, and for your consistent support and belief in me, not only in this journey of writing my book, but in so many other respects. As a valued professional and good friend, your support has meant the world to me while writing my book.

Ken Haumann, you have been a rock and a pillar for me, as a friend and a confidant, in everything that I do. You have always told me that I have many books in me that the world needs to read, and now you won't get to see the finished product. You left this world too soon, and I miss you daily. Thank you for your love and support; your voice has echoed in my mind at times when I needed inspiration to continue. Thank you for the blessing of having you in my life and in my heart.

Suzanne Stevens, as founder of YouMeWe Social Impact Group, and as a very successful social entrepreneur, your time, insights and our valuable conversations have contributed greatly to my understanding of the needs of female entrepreneurs in Canada, and has been inspiring. Thank you for your support and contribution in my journey as I was writing my book.

Derek De Beer, thank you for your generosity of spirit and your inspiring stories that you have so freely shared with me. Your life in the music business has demonstrated to me that no industry is immune to connectedness, and it has helped me to reflect on different concepts from various perspectives while writing the book; I thank you for this.

Judy Robinett, you are an international business woman with heart and fire; you have achieved so much and have taken so many people with you along the road. From our very first time we spoke and since, you have been an example to me of how I want to show up as a business woman—strong yet gentle, smart yet principled, driven yet inclusive. I appreciate your continued advice, support and guidance, and I am grateful for the privilege of calling you a mentor and a friend. When I had to dig deeper into my consciousness, to extract my book from my soul and put it onto paper, at times I would ask myself: "What would Judy do?"

Ashley Paulse, thank you very much for the conversations that we have shared, and the insights you have provided me with your confluence of spiritual, family, social and business pursuits that are vested in the African Ubuntu ideology and in your Cooperative Movement in South Africa. It was a delight to learn about these aspects and your view on connectivity as I wrote my book.

Vishen Lakhiani, you and your MindValley organisation have turned the world upside down, or shall I say right side up, when it comes to education and learning in our new world. You are a part of my life daily as you bring education and learning from all corners of the world into my home and onto my phone. Your life story acts as an inspiration to me, that I too can achieve the great things I am meant to achieve in life. I aspire to be one of your MindValley educators in the future, and I am looking forward to that moment when I get to work alongside you, even if for a fleeting moment, in service of humanity. Thank you for never giving up on your dreams, for stretching and persevering to build a connected world in learning. Your business model is the epiphany of a realised leadership currency in action!!

To both **Ivan Cash and TedX,** I want to thank you for making very valuable examples, of success in collaboration, available to people through the powerful platform of TedX. Ivan, your beautiful and practical example inspired me to continue writing my book. It is so powerful in illustrating that not only can we use the power of connectedness in any field to make an impact, but also in an

For bonuses go to ...

increasingly divided and digital world; it shows that human connection is more important than ever.

Jack Ma, you are a living example of the power of connectivity and community in your great business success in building Alibaba. Your approach to business and relationships provided me with a lot of insight while writing my book.

Linda Hill, I want to acknowledge and thank you for the message that you consistently share and demonstrate to the world, in regard to the power of collaboration. Whether it be in leading change and innovation, or developing innovative ecosystems, you continue to show the world the power of collective genius. Some of your teachings have inspired and intensified my understanding and expression of the value of community, collaboration and connectedness, which has informed sections of my book.

Shanda Sumpter, you and your HeartCore team have been instrumental in me getting my book written. Your approach to business, the coaching you have provided to me, and your virtual services empowered me to take action to interview key people that informed parts of my book. You continue to inspire me as a successful business woman with heart. You lead with giving, which is true to my ethos. I aspire to work in closer proximity with you in the future. Thank you for the gift of you.

Eckhart Tolle, I would like to deeply thank you for the wisdom and influence that you have brought into my life through your books, videos, discussions and other media. I have held on to several of your quotes through different experiences in my life, like: "Some changes look negative on the surface, but you will soon realize that space is being created in your life for something new to emerge." I truly appreciate who you are.

www.connectedrainmaker.com

Oprah Winfrey, your life's work continuously inspires me to try harder, work more, and stretch and grow more, so that I can serve more, impact more and bring richness to other people's lives. Thank you for being an example to me of how a powerful, authentic message shared with others, can bring great meaning to them. Your example has encouraged me to write my book, and to share a message of looking within, finding the gift of caring and sharing, and building connections—tapestries of collaboration—to co-elevate the world.

Reese Witherspoon, your drive for standing up for what you believe in, giving women a voice and an opportunity in the entertainment industry, has been very inspirational to me. At times when I needed a bit of encouragement to persist, watching a video clip of your drive and your persistence helped me to get going again. Thank you for leading by example.

Karl Nurenberg, thank you so much for your generosity of spirit, and for taking the time to guide me in regard to how I can get my message to the most amount of people in the best possible way. You are directly contributing to my success of sharing and impacting many people around the world.

Danette May, the story that you shared of how you stood up like a phoenix from the ashes, from a very difficult setting, succeeding to become the vibrant woman you are today, has been an inspiration for me in my journey of immigration. The path was not always easy, but courageous women like yourself have made it easier for me to stay focused on my goals and dreams, and to persist in serving people globally.

Michelle Obama, you are an inspiration, not only to me but to many aspiring women leaders. Thank you for the time, love, guidance and support that you bring to so many of us, showing us that we can make a difference with and through other people, to contribute on a large scale.

For bonuses go to ...

South Africa High Commission (Ottawa), Ms. Sibongiseni Dlamini-Mntambo, I want to acknowledge you for the work you do in bridging continuous interest for connections and bridge building between Canada and South Africa, and in so doing, contributing to the building of co-elevated teams that can impact many people across the globe.

John Saikaley, you are a business leader with heart, in the insurance industry. When I arrived in Canada a few years ago, I knew no one, and it took time to build the trust and the authentic relationships required to make a meaningful impact in Canada. I want to thank you for being one of the first people to help me selflessly, asking for nothing in return. You exemplify the 5 Steps that I teach in this book, and I want to thank you for your professional support and your friendship since then.

Edith Rowberry and Vianney Gemme, thank you very much for being like my family in Canada. The privilege to know that you are there for me through thick and thin, has been a huge support for me, and I want to deeply thank you for your love, support and encouragement to follow my dreams.

Charles Wachsberg, you and your team at Apollo are exemplary of the principles that I lay out in my book. It is a privilege to call you a business partner, and I thank you for being an example of a leader that leads through relationships—may your impact continue to grow from strength to strength.

Rochelle Miller, you are a critical part of my soul family. I want to thank and acknowledge you for the immense value, guidance, support and direction that you continue to bring into my life. It is a heavenly blessing to be connected to you.

Rotary International, you are an organisation that has encouraged collaboration and relationships for over a century. Thank you for bringing together business and professional leaders in order to provide

www.connectedrainmaker.com

humanitarian service, and to advance goodwill and peace around the world; this is exactly what my book focuses on—the power and impact of connections.

Simon Sinek, I have the highest respect for your ability to articulate yourself so impactfully, and I appreciate your mind and way of thinking. Your perspectives of how relationships should make us grow or make us a better version of ourselves, were aspects that I pondered as inspiration to some of the chapters I wrote in this book. Thank you for your contribution to my growth, and for helping me to be a better version of myself by listening to you and your perspectives.

Business Networking International (BNI), as the world's largest referral networking organization, you help businesses to be a part of a local network with global reach. Your work supports the building of co-elevated teams that lead to higher and faster impact. This is the message that I bring to leaders in my book, and I thank you for playing such an important role in facilitating authentic connections.

The Networker (Toronto), you are a network of networks, and your objective of seeking to connect business people across Toronto is beautifully aligned with the philosophies that I highlight in my book. Thank you for the great work that you do in supporting Canadian businesses to collaborate and succeed.

SUCCESS **magazine and SUCCESS.com,** you inform and support new and established leaders to understand and value the fact that they are empowered to control their own destiny. I have read your magazine since I was a young woman, and it has greatly enriched me with advice, best business practices and inspiration from major business personalities, which has contributed to my growth and development as a business woman. Thank you for your contribution in shaping me to share my book with the world.

For bonuses go to ...

Kim Elliot and **Libby Davies** thank you for your willingness to assist and advise me with regards to positioning, marketing and creating visibility for my mission through this book.

Bruce Campbell thank you for your valuable time, input and guidance, and for your willingness to review my book with the intent to position it to serve and make a difference in Canada and North America.

Grant Cardone your ability to scale a business is phenomenal, and you also emphasise the importance of a team of people to reach high level impact. I have learnt a lot from you and want to thank you for the growth that you have contributed to in me, this has prepared me to embark on projects like writing this book with success.

Anik Singal and LURN you are phenomenal, you have shown me the power of relationships in the digital world, thank you for the lessons I have learnt from you that have inspired aspects of my book.

Russ Ruffino and ENTRE, your dedication to people – and more specifically serving others, and your focus on community, while building business success is inspirational, and I thank you for the privilege of being part of your community.

Gerhard Kotze, Roy Fine and **Roland Buhler**, you have been a very strong alliance and trusted business partners for a long time. Thank you for the privilege of living the principles in my book as a collective, and for the difference we have been able to make in various communities as a result.

ANB, Ron Stubbs and **Bruce Longlade** thank you for the opportunity to continue working with you in Canada in the OTC and Wellness space, in such a collaborative way. You demonstrate the principles that I speak of in this book, in your approach to business and I wanted to acknowledge you.

www.connectedrainmaker.com

Ken Blanchard since I have been a young girl, yourself and Nelson Mandela have been an inspiration to me about what true leadership looks like. You are really impacting the world through your devotion to teaching servant leadership through the power of love rather than the love of power. I continue to strive to live my life by these principles, and I would like to thank you for what this has meant to me and the many leaders I have taught and coached in my life on your principle of servant leadership.

Asia Africa Forum on Corruption (AAFC), Kusuma Chandra and **Rahul Singh** it is rewarding to be an advisor for Africa to your association, and its reassuring to see how you engage through authentic relationships to promote transparency and limited corruption in Asia and Africa regions.

Telfer School of Management and **OttawaU** I would like to thank you for the contribution that you make to the business community in Canada, you understand the importance of building tight-knit communities that make up your management school and that contribute in the business of building a better Canada.

Southern African Venture Capital and Private Equity Association (SAVCA) and **Tanya Van Lill**, your association depicts the framework of collaboration and creating high impact co-elevated teams of expertise, that I refer to in my book. Thank you for our partnership and for the gift of serving your members alongside you.

L'Université du Québec à Montréal (UQAM) and **Benoit Chalifoux** thank you for believing in me and giving me a platform to serve Canadian leaders when I just arrived in Canada, when no other Canadian University was open to doing this at the time. Your spirit of collaboration and your approach to serving as communities is the new way to prepare our future leaders to make a meaningful impact in the new world of work.

For bonuses go to ...

Professor Jagdish Sheth as a renowned scholar and recognised thought leader you have been inspirational to me. Thank you for taking the time to have discussions with me and share your thought, insights and wisdom, as I was writing my book.

Ambassador Omar Arouna I regard you as a partner in bridging the collaborative interests of USA and the continent of Africa. You are an example of the type of connected leadership I refer to in my book, and I appreciate you.

Linda Fitzgerald and your podcast (Serendipity Stories) thank you for featuring me as part of your first podcast series. You understand the principle of collaboration, and I wish you great success.

Kaduna Business School and **Dahiru Sani** we have had a long-term relationship in serving African leaders. I thank you for all the rich experiences that we have had together while serving alongside each other, some of these experiences have formed part of the series of stories I have shared in my book.

Professor Koos Koen you were my first business partner that showed me the possibilities of co-elevated collaboration. Our business partnership was my first experience as an entrepreneur where I applied the business principles that have been the cornerstone of my book, I am deeply grateful to you, I will always love and care about you deeply.

Maurice Jonker you are a valued friend and I want to thank you for volunteering to support me and offer me advise, give feedback on editorial components, share your views and opinions to help me strengthen my value offering, all of this contributed greatly during the writing of my book.

Doug Power you are an example of a Canadian business leader that understands the power and value of connections. I appreciate our

www.connectedrainmaker.com

collaborative relationship, and I look forward to the impact we will continue to make as a collective in Canada. You live the principles I speak of in my book.

Andre Moolman your openness to collaborative partnerships, the high level of trust and reliability that you bring into a business alliance is a powerful example of exactly what I share as a model in my book. Thank you for reviewing my book, and for sharing your ideas on how to reach the most people with this message of leading with generosity towards the greater good of all.

Dempsey Naidoo you have been an example to me of the power of collaborative partnerships and the value of relationships for most of my young leadership life. Thank you for our new business partnership in Canada, this opportunity forms part of the foundation of my connector business model in action.

Foundation Fuel and **Indrajit Gupta** thank you for the opportunity to collaborate, and for creating a platform for me to share my insights and teachings from this book, globally

Intersol, Marc Valois and the **rest of the team** it is a pleasure to collaborate with you in Canada, to serve the businesses and associations that provide the services to our people. Your work ethics and approach to clients are aligned with the principles I share in this book, thank you for being another powerful example of the value of connections.

The Canada Africa Chamber of Business, Garreth Bloor and **Jacques NdoutouMvé** the work you do in bridging collaborative opportunities for Canada and the African continent is so incredibly important. I thank you for inviting me into your community to serve together, and for the platform that you have offered me to practise the principles I share in my book.

For bonuses go to ...

Trisha Fraley you are such a special person, my first significant experience of the power of virtual collaborative relationships, an unforgettable experience. I also want to thank you for the support that you are providing me to launch my book, and market it online.

Drew Thacker thank you for telling me to go for it, and just write my book. You told me that I have a few books inside of me, you have always believed in me, and for this I thank you.

Conscious Enterprise Network (CEN), Dominique Conterno and **Esther Robles** from the first time we met we knew we were kindred spirits. Your CEN Network is an example of a very powerful collaborative community. Thank you for the opportunity to have strategically aligned with you and for inviting me to share my message with the world through your platform.

Marisa Peer the transformational work that you do has been a very important part of my daily habits, offering me the mental support and so much more while I was writing my book. You continue to have a significant impact on my life.

Jackee Batanda you are exemplary of what it takes to be a good writer, thank you for the encouragement and support you have offered me in my journey as I have authored this book.Thank you to my many terrific **field partners**, my valued **business relationships and partners** (you know who you are), whom I know will be helping me create a lot of connected communities that will drive impact and wealth creation for a lot of people, for many years to come. You and the work we do together, inspires me to work daily on being a better version of myself, and to continue to build the co-elevated communities that can bring global solutions to global problems, and in so doing, uplift the experience of living on Mother Earth for everyone.

www.connectedrainmaker.com

I am very grateful to every member of my **African Rainmaker Community**, who have trusted me to mentor and coach them on their various routes to leadership success. Continue to shine your light.

Chapter 1

How My Connected Story Began

The Power of the Spirit of Ubuntu

"Love is a game that two can play and both win."
— Eva Gabor

My story started in a beautiful world heritage site in Africa, a small town that is part of the Zulu Kingdom. In the heart of Kwa Zulu Natal, something very special was about to happen. Two influential men from the community, one of them being the community doctor, and the other being the chief of the Zulus, were about to have a great blessing bestowed upon each of them—the birth of their very first child.

It is important to understand that this was the time of apartheid in South Africa, so the story has greater meaning embedded than you could maybe imagine. The story plays out between two very unlikely friends, and the only reason for this friendship was because of the Power of Love, the Power of Relationships, and the Power of Connectedness, which was much stronger than the Power of Forced Regulations, Forced Rules and Forced Separation, Discrimination and Isolation. You see, these two men that I am referring to were supposedly on opposite sides of the fence, invisibly divided as black and white. But love and their need to connect, because of their shared love and belief in the power of community that ran through their collective veins, was stronger than the enforced ideation of separation, "apartheid."

So these two men were connected in a significant way. The doctor, being my father, had a vision to serve and heal, not only a select few but the whole community. So he reached out to the chief to ask for his permission to serve in the Zulu community as a healer, and to exchange best practice, teach and learn from the traditional Zulu tribal healers. Over a period of time, they started building a relationship; and this relationship, unbeknownst to either of them, would become a very strong foundation for healing and for unity in an environment that was legislatively governed for separation. Thanks to my father, I would get to witness the magical power held in, what we call in Africa, the Spirit of Ubuntu. You see, there is a Zulu proverb called Ubuntu that says: "I am a person through other people."

Archbishop Desmond Tutu explained it in this way: "One of the sayings in our country is Ubuntu—the essence of being human. Ubuntu speaks particularly about the fact that you can't exist as a human being in isolation." Ubuntu means love, truth, peace, happiness, eternal optimism, inner goodness, etc. Ubuntu is the essence of a human being, the divine spark of goodness inherent within each being. From the beginning of time, the divine principles of Ubuntu have guided African societies, and they were also guiding my father and the chief.

My father was no ordinary man; he was divinely favoured, favoured with a heart filled with love, compassion and the true sense of giving and healing, and so he understood that in Zulu culture, even if your intent is to help, you do not just walk into a community and start spreading the word. No, you first build a relationship with the chief, out of respect, and you show him your pure intent. And once you have his blessing, he will invite you into the community. The chief, being a wise man himself, quickly recognised the special spark in my father, and so they became friends. What endeared them to each other even more, was this special experience they would share, of both of them expecting their first born child, at more or less the same time. One of the children I'm referring to was, of course, me.

My beautiful mother and wonderful father had very excitedly started discussing what they would name their baby once he or she was born. During those years, there were no machines to determine the gender of the baby in advance, so they had to make provision for the possibility of a boy's name and a girl's name, while waiting for me to arrive.

What's in a Name?

> *"What's in a name? That which we call a rose by any other name would smell as sweet."*
> – William Shakespeare

I was born in South Africa, in the spring; I'm African. In Africa, we often have a Western name and an African name, so my full name is Ezanne Nomvula Swanepoel. My Western name was given to me by my parents in a slightly different way than usual. I am from the subculture, Afrikaans. And in Afrikaans culture, what we have a tendency to do, like in Europe, possibly because of our heritage from Europe through colonisation, is that the oldest daughter or the oldest son—so, the firstborn—is usually given family names. During this discussion between my parents, of name selections, my mother said to my father that she was not so sure about this tradition of naming their child after the grandmother or grandfather, because they typically had such long names, like Stefannes Johannes, or Susanna Gertruida... And then you would just call the child Stef or Gertie as the shortened version. She did not want her children to carry the burden of these long names, and rather wanted to give them beautiful, original names, something unique. My father was a little bit more traditional. And he wasn't sure; he didn't want to rock the boat with the family, because I was not only their first child, but I was also the very first grandchild on both my

For bonuses go to ...

mother's and my father's sides of the family. Everyone was watching to see what they were going to do.

My parents came to an agreement that if it was a son, they would call their son after my father's family names. If it was a daughter, my mother said that then she would like their daughter to be called Ezanne. It was an original name that she created, taking inspiration from my grandmother's name, Elizabeth Anne. What my mother did was to take the E and Z from Elizabeth, and ANNE, and it became EZANNE. Ezanne, the name, had no meaning, no meaning at all. It was just a beautiful, original creation as my mother had wished for, and she liked the sound of the name. Eventually, the wait was over, and I was born. We now know that I was a girl; my parents went ahead, as they had agreed, and gave me the name Ezanne.

At the same time, the chief and my father would check in with each other from time to time during their wives' pregnancies, speaking a lot to each other about the births of their first children...they were on this exciting adventure together. And just before my birth, it was a time of drought in our province, Kwa-Zulu Natal. Some of you might want to Google some of the things I share in the story, because this might not be common knowledge for everyone reading this. See below, a map to give you a general idea of the geographic location.

www.connectedrainmaker.com

Know that Kwa-Zulu Natal is an evergreen area, a subtropical climate; very seldom is there any drought. But in this instance, just before my birth, there was a huge drought. The Zulus did everything they could think of in order to make it rain. Traditionally, they did rain dances, they prayed to their ancestors—they did all kinds of different things— but no rain arrived. And then, at the moment that I was born, it started raining, and it rained in a way that we call, in Zulu, "khiza," which is a very soft drizzle; it is very nourishing, and plants and vegetation can sprout very quickly. This was something phenomenal to the Zulus; it also meant that the cattle would be saved, because there was food for them to eat. Zulus view cattle as a sacred animal, and cattle also represent the wealth of the tribe. Therefore, they viewed my birth, along with the gift of rain, as a sacred symbol or blessing. The chief got word to my father that the ancestors had given me an African name, and that I was gifted with the name Nomvula. For those of you that don't know, this translates literally to mean "Queen of the Rain," so yes, you're in the presence of royalty. Nice to meet you…ha ha.

So you might be asking why I'm sharing this with you. It will become clearer in a moment…

The Large Whiskey Bottle

"If I'm gonna tell a real story, I'm gonna start with my name."
—Kendrick Lamar

Very often, in relationships or connections, we like to point out differences, but we actually have a lot of similarities as human beings, even in different subcultures, if we just take the time to notice them. At the time in question, it seemed unlikely, but my father realised that in Zulu and Afrikaans culture, there were some important similarities, one of these being that the birth of the firstborn is an important event within the extended family environment. Historically, it has been customary for both Afrikaner and Zulu married couples to name their

For bonuses go to ...

first son after the husband's father, and their first daughter after the wife's mother. And although my father, till his dying day, denied it, another similarity between Zulu and Afrikaans culture at the given time in question, was that if the first born was a son, it had a little bit more significance than if it was a daughter as the firstborn. So, a little bit more priority was given if the firstborn was a son. The role of the firstborn child has thus been socially significant, particularly for a firstborn son in patriarchal societies. For Zulu traditionalists, it would even go a step further; childlessness or giving birth to girls only, was a sign of the greatest of all misfortunes, and no marriage would be permanent in Zulu culture, until a child, especially a boy, was born, which made the birth of a boy in Zulu culture significantly more important.

Now please understand that my father loved my sisters and me dearly, and I don't think he would have exchanged us for anything, but I always used to tease him about the importance of a boy versus a girl, because just before my birth, he was given a gift by a very good friend of his, Bing Rabe. And this gift was a 4.5 litre bottle of whiskey—for its time, a very good quality whiskey—and a very, very large bottle at that. If you want to see a photo of the infamous whiskey bottle, just go to www.connectedrainmaker.com, and you can download your full-size, full-colour, print-ready copy of the bottle.

Quickly, the idea was formulated between my father and his friends, that they were going to drink the whole bottle together as a community of brothers, to celebrate the birth of the boy. Evidently, when I was born, I was not a boy, so the infamous large bottle of good quality whiskey remained closed.

And then the second and the third child was born, both also daughters, and the bottle remained closed. So, whenever my father and I had this conversation, I would tease him and I would say, "Daddy, the bottle of whiskey is still closed? So how can it not be that a little bit more importance is given to having a boy than a girl?" And I'm sure he's laughing at me in heaven right now. That is the way it was.

So that bottle of whiskey is still standing there on his iconic bar, in our family home in South Africa, and will probably never be opened. I don't know what occasion would break the code so that it could be opened, because even the first grandson and granddaughter has since been born, and it still has not been opened. The opening of the old, large whiskey bottle remains a mystery for the immediate future...

This brings us back to the relevance of a name. In ancient African culture, names held a mesmerizing mystique. This makes selecting names extra important, because to some extent, the individual will come to embody their namesake. It is therefore believed that the chosen names carry great influence over a child's life and that of their family...still, I did not fully understand how my name, Ezanne Nomvula, would have an influence, or how it would express my destiny; that is until two special events happened, and the puzzle pieces started to make more sense to me. Let me share the missing pieces with you!

A Destiny Announced at Birth

> *"There are two great days in a person's life*
> *—the day we are born and the day we discover why."*
> – William Barclay

Approximately 13 years ago, I was in Marseille, France, with some of my colleagues during an international seminar, which I have been invited to over the last 15 years bi-annually, to coach and prepare some of the top business school students entering the business world, from Kedge Business School. There was a gentleman from America that was part of the expert group, and when we introduced ourselves to each other, he said to me that he knew Africans have a meaning to the name they are given at birth, and he wanted to know the meaning of my name. I explained to him that my African name meant "Queen of the Rain." His response was almost immediate, "Oh, something like the Rainmaker." And that stuck from there onwards...today still, I am known as the African Rainmaker.

I do not know if you know what "the Rainmaker" means. From an American perspective, it usually symbolizes a person who brings clients, business and money to the business environment or firm, and could also mean a person with a large following and the ability to raise funds for others. As mentioned earlier, in African tradition, when we get our name at birth, this is a very important ceremony, because we believe that the name that you are given at birth has a very big contribution to your purpose, your contribution, in this world. In other words, your destiny. So this was an interesting concept for me...the person that "brings clients, business and money, and has a large following." So this was my African name...initially, the meaning of it was hard to digest in terms of contribution. And it was only when I was able to put together the meaning of my African and Western names, that I better understood what my purpose and destiny held.

My Western name, Ezanne, as I had mentioned to you, was my beautiful mother's creation, and it didn't have any particular meaning, or this was at least what I thought at the time...that is until I had the opportunity to work with important leaders in Nigeria. Have you been to Nigeria, or at least know where Nigeria is? In case you have not had the pleasure to visit this complex and interesting country, Nigeria is in the western part of Africa. I had to go and assist some of the Nigerian leaders as a strategic advisor and facilitator; they were in a new election year. They had realised that they needed to make some changes in Nigeria.

Just in case you haven't been to Nigeria, it's important to understand that at the time, Nigeria and its approach to leadership was viewed as slightly militant in its leadership approach. And the leadership realised that if they wanted to be competitive globally, they needed to make sure that the leadership was a little bit more open to the global business world of doing things. But they knew that culturally they couldn't just suddenly change the way that they lead; the people of the country would just vote them out, which would mean that they would have no positive contribution or impact. So instead, what they did was to call me as a strategic advisor to assist them to build a new or adjusted way in which they could lead, that would retain the respect of their people, and support the country's economic development to have more impact globally—which today, from an African standpoint, it certainly has.

Anyone heard about Nollywood? Incidentally, Nollywood is the film industry in Nigeria, and is in fact the second largest movie industry globally in terms of output, producing about 2,500 films in a year. This number surpasses Hollywood and is second only to India's Bollywood. Nigeria still has a few other challenges to overcome; but economically, they definitely are going in the right direction, so our experience together was certainly worth it. Another part of the Nigerian culture is that when you form a bond with a Nigerian family or business unit, they would usually bless you with an African name. This created excitement in me, because I could feel our relationship growing over the time we were working together, and I was looking forward to the opportunity to get my African name.

Soon came the time for us to say our goodbyes, and during our farewell ritual, no one gave me an African name. I was disappointed, and so I said, "Guys, are we not close? Why did you not give me an African name?" They were surprised by my response and said: "But you already have an African name." At the time, I thought they were referring to Nomvula, my Zulu name, so I said, "Yes, but that's a Zulu name. It's not a Nigerian name." And they said, "No, Ezanne, you have an African Nigerian name." And I was confused; I only knew my two names: Ezanne and Nomvula.

For bonuses go to ...

Now, what I didn't say to you earlier was that they always pronounced my name, Ezanne, slightly differently to what I was used to. I just thought it was due to their different accent, and never corrected anyone; I would just respond to the newly found pronunciation of my name Ezanne, because I really didn't mind. But at this stage of our conversation, they explained to me that Ezanne was an Igbo word, which is one of the two most spoken languages in Nigeria. Igbo (also called Ibo) people live chiefly in southeastern Nigeria, and they speak Igbo, a language of the Benue-Congo branch of the Niger-Congo language family. Igbo is the second most populous indigenous language of southern Nigeria, spoken by about 25 million people. They had made a slight alteration to the spelling of my name, to "Ezinne," but the pronunciation of both remained the same. This word, "Ezinne," means "the good mother," and they added, "the good mother of Africa."

The Bridge Builder Serving Humanity

*"What I do is the opposite of building walls. I build bridges.
A bridge is something that connects instead of separating."*
— Santiago Calatrava

This was a huge blessing and a huge responsibility gifted to me; you see, a naming ritual in the African context is significant. And I realised that if this was true, that our names dictate what we bring to this world at birth, it meant that I was the good mother of Africa, who brings clients, business and money, and has a large following. This made me reflect deeply: What road had my life led me on to this point, and what did this mean for the road ahead?

Some parts of the meaning, I already understood, because I had subsequently already started to bring clients, business, relationships and money to projects and business opportunities between Africa and the rest of the world. And this is something that naturally progressed in my career. So I could clearly understand how that was linked to my purpose. But the other part, being the good mother of Africa, took me a while to understand what it meant. Today, my understanding is that one of the critical functions of the mother in a family is to make sure that the family communicates and collaborates, and that they take care to make sure that the relationships stay strong, that people get together, and that they work together and help each other. So it is almost like a bridging function—bringing people, families and communities together, and also strengthening the love they feel for each other.

And so, when I look at what I've done in business, that's exactly what I've been doing for a very long time. I have been privileged to really serve as a strategic adviser and a coach to some of the most prominent companies, country leaders, entrepreneurs, executive teams, CEOs and even royal families in Africa, and I've helped them to transform their teams and their networks in order for them to transform the very world we live in every day, for the future and for the betterment of society, and I have supported the bridging and bridge building between different stakeholders in business. If you want to know more about my coaching and consulting services I offer to business leaders and businesses, please feel free to go to www.connectedrainmaker.com for more information.

Of course, it wasn't always like that; it happened organically over time. And I started at the bottom and worked my way up, slowly but surely, to the top leaders that wanted to get my advice and my support to assist them. Because ultimately, we need to be connected with the right people to be able to provide a larger impact faster. This is what I want to share with you—how you can do this too—and it starts with just knowing yourself a bit better, having self-awareness. In this book, I will talk to you about how we actually put together true, generous and authentic relationships that serve you in business, and that serve you in life moving forward. So please don't feel overwhelmed or nervous...you'd be surprised at how many of these leaders that I've

For bonuses go to ...

referred to, feel a bit nervous or apprehensive themselves at times to engage with people that they don't know. It is our intent that leads us, and that starts with ourselves, knowing what you stand for and what you want to contribute in this world. If you are wondering about what you really want in life, you can go to www.connected rainmaker.com. I offer a programme that you would benefit greatly from; it helps you design what you want in all 12 areas of your life—a clear life plan of what you want, customised specifically for you.

Now, I know that many of you reading this book might feel more comfortable and confident online to engage with people. But the part that I think we can get more support in, is that once you've engaged with people online, that transfers into face-to-face connection and coming across authentically and confidently so that you can follow through and follow up. Otherwise, there's a limitation in the value that the mutual relationship can bring. And so, this is not unique to you. It's not unique to those other leaders, and it includes me too. We sometimes have limiting belief systems that hold us back in order to go through this process. This is a large part of where I can bring value to your life, I know how to do this. I've done it for myself, and I have learnt the shortcuts over time. I wish someone had taken the time to share with me, what I will be sharing with you over the course of our time together. It is time for us to drive with intent and impact, and to do it through bridging, collaboration and through co-elevated approaches. You don't have to learn the hard way or the long way, through only your own experiences. Instead, you can learn from my experience to fast track yourself onto a road of collective impact and fulfilment. You're going to learn exactly how to access the right people, in the right way—not in a way that you feel that you are using people, but in a way that you're building relationships, so that there's mutual exchange and mutual value.

The Global Citizen

> *"Respect is how you treat everyone,
> not just those you want to impress."*
> – Richard Branson

You might be meeting people and thinking, based on certain preconceived ideas that you have, that they are this way or they are that way. But you see, you never know. You never know, when you engage with someone, what their real story is. Where do they come from? What is the richness in that human being? One piece of advice I'd like to share with you, is to just decide whether you want to be respectful to everyone or disrespectful to everyone. And I'm not going to tell you which one you must choose. But what I'd like to encourage you to do is to make a decision and treat everyone the way in which you've decided—don't treat one person different to another based on what you think you can get from them. because it never works out. People can see through that consistency or inconsistency; in whatever way you make your choice, that is where the value is going to be for you.

This is part of why I wanted to share something personal with you, something real about me, by sharing the life story and significance of my name. I'm not going to bring you textbook answers. I want to help you be prepared for the real world, to have a *global citizen mindset*. My wish for you is to have the ability to access what it means to be a real leader in the real world, and to make a real impact on other humans. We can learn certain facts in textbooks, but the rest is not black and white. There's not a right and a wrong. And that's the difficulty of being a leader in today's world; there are very often different versions of the truth. And it's about understanding how to work through those to be respectful and inclusive of other people when you make your decisions. So how does that sound as a starting point? Do I have your commitment that you will use this as an

For bonuses go to www.connectedrainmaker.com

opportunity of discovery, and being open to challenge yourself and your current thinking?

I have been very blessed in my life, and I never take this for granted. I have shared experiences with very interesting and empowered people, like having a cup of coffee with Donna Karan from DKNY to discuss a project she was doing at the time in Haiti, assisting in a community upliftment project through using her talent and experience in design and fashion, and I wanted to explore if there would be opportunities for us to do some similar projects on the African continent. You know by now that I am a huge supporter of collaboration, but be sure that most people that create impact, are also collaborators by nature. The fashion world is one of those environments that loves collaboration, and often it's even better when they're executed with altruistic intentions. That's exactly the case for Kenneth Cole and Donna Karan, notable American designers who have, since my discussion with Donna, teamed up over their shared love for Haiti.

Gentle Souls, Kenneth Cole's shoe line that prioritises comfort, and Urban Zen, Donna Karan's lifestyle brand, released a shoe collection not too long ago. The pair designed the collection on a trip to Haiti, and hired local artisans to make the shoes by hand. Their ultimate goal has been to promote Haiti's artisan culture and create jobs, and their long-time collaborator, Pascale Théard, made this vision come to life with the help of her team of talented leather workers, embroiderers, designers, sewers and shoemakers. Can you see the power of authentic collaboration? (If you want to see the photo of Donna Karan and me, please go to www.connectedrainmaker.com.) This is a business community at work.

The road we are embarking on together through this book, is globally transferable, so it does not matter where you find yourself right now, or how big or how small you feel, the process can work for you. Let's go to the next chapter to learn more about why the time is now to focus on your relationship currency.

Chapter 2

Why Tell the Story Now?

Standing on the Backs of Giants

> *"Surround yourself with only people who are going to lift you higher."*
> – Oprah Winfrey

As I share my story and the experiences I have had in my life to date, you will realise that the principles that I am sharing with you are not new to me; they have been foundational to how I live my life. I have had the opportunity to work in over 30 countries across 5 continents, and in total have travelled to more than 100 countries.

So, you might be wondering why I have decided to share this information now, and not earlier, or maybe at a later point in life. Well, the global impact of COVID certainly has had something to do with it, but it's not the whole story...in fact, I think these principles have been important for a very long time, and it's just that only a select few— the top 1 to 2% of successful people—were aware of the power of relationships or connections, and its ability to impact significantly and secretly, being the real leadership currency.

For bonuses go to ...

There are a handful of things that separate the ultra-rich from everyone else: research has shown they tend to exercise regularly, maintain a healthy diet, save 10% or more of their income, read books and manage their time wisely. But the most important—and the most overlooked—habit they share that helped them grow their wealth, in large part, is their commitment to forge valuable relationships with selected individuals. It's human nature to associate ourselves with likeminded people with whom we feel the most comfortable. The ultra-wealthy and successful, however, are a lot more selective about who they allow into their inner circle. Nearly all the self-made millionaires that have been interviewed by various people have said that one of their top priorities was cultivating "rich relationships" and avoiding the "toxic" ones. It's important to note that a "rich relationship" is defined by mindset rather than by wealth. In other words, individuals who contribute to rich relationships don't necessarily have big bank accounts, but they all have lofty goals and aspirations—and they spend much of their time trying to achieve them.

Warren Buffet once said that one will move in the direction of the people that you associate with, and billionaires Warren Buffet and Bill Gates have agreed that by choosing the right group of friends, you can push yourself to achieve bigger professional goals. Lastly, Richard Branson, another billionaire that we can learn from, who has more than 400 companies, said that you can't do good business with a bad person. He highlights that you need to find the right people to work with, and then you can't go wrong. He also said that through the right people focusing on the right things, we can, in time, get on top of a lot, if not most, of the problems of this world, and that's what a number of us are doing. The new formula for business success is to build companies as communities.

When I became aware of some statistics, thanks to studies done during COVID, I realised that it is my duty to share what I know with you, someone that wants to make a difference and bring meaning to this world by using your talents to serve others and empower yourself and your loved ones. It is my duty to share some of the secrets and tips that have been known to only a few, about how through authentic meaningful relationships, we can truly serve faster to larger numbers of people, which also means more value contribution back to you, because we are all rewarded in the same and equal proportion to the extent to which we impact and serve. So, the greater the impact and service, the greater the reward for you.

COVID Shook Me to Action

"Cross the river in a crowd, and the crocodile won't eat you."
– African proverb

I will share some statistics from the COVID pandemic with you, to show you that consistently feeling connected—in other words, relationships—is something that has become really important, especially during the time of COVID, or at least the realisation of the role that relationships play, because it has always been important. All of these studies have been done in 2020 during COVID.

A study by the Harvard Business Review said that since the outbreak of the pandemic, they did research with people that were primarily employees. A lot of them of course were working from home, and 70% of employees were in the USA, so this was primarily a Harvard Business Review focused on the impact on Americans; still, there is relevance as a guide, no matter where you are living on the globe. They said 75% of employees had expressed that they feel socially isolated. Imagine that 57% of them also said that they felt greater anxiety. Think back; how did you experience this unprecedented event? Did you feel more anxiety; did it create social isolation for you? Further to this, 53% of people said they felt more emotionally exhausted. This boded the question as to why people gained more anxiety or felt emotionally more exhausted when they felt socially isolated. What we realised was that in most cases, isolation created more stressful people.

Forbes also gave some statistics in regard to research studied and completed, and 20% of remote employees said that they lacked a sense of belonging, and sometimes felt really lonely. Now, what we know from previous research in a lot of psychological reviews, is that as soon as someone feels that they don't belong—in other words, they have no purpose—we start seeing other things happen, like suicide rates increase, and depression increases, and these kinds of things have a very negative effect on our community and our civilization. Can you see how much more important it is now for us to actively seek out relationships?

If you need more facts, well, National Law Review, in 2020, also said that 45% of adults were reporting that anxiety and stress related to COVID-19 had a very negative impact on their mental health. Can you see that if people feel a lack of sense of belonging, or they feel isolated or alone, that psychologically it can have a mental impact too? And remember, this is not something that we have a tendency to admit; very often, we feel we need to be stronger. So, if 45% of people were willing to admit it, I think the statistics are probably even higher in practice.

In this scenario, if there is good news, this is the good news, and there is one thing that those people that were managing really well, or much better—let me say much better than most people—had in common... it wasn't power...a lot of people think that if you're in power, you might feel better, but no. CEOs, executives, wealthy people, celebrities—all of them fit into those statistics, but it wasn't power. We might think, okay, if you have a lot of money, then COVID is easier for you and better for you, because at least you can pay all your obligations. But no, some of the wealthiest people were also very, very worried, and had high stress levels. It wasn't having perceived control either. The only thing that made people manage better—that everyone that was managing COVID better had in common—was this one thing: the presence of long-term, well-established and meaningful relationships. So, in other words, people that stood with them or behind them, or said in another way, people that felt that they had someone in their life that had their back—in essence, the sense of a feeling of belonging to a community. So this might bode a very pertinent question: Who has your back?

Who Has My Back?

> *"To be without a friend is to be poor indeed."*
> – Tanzanian proverb

Looking at the statistics and how people have been impacted, made me think a lot about European versus African versus North American versus Asian culture. It was very interesting to me because, in Africa, and certainly in South Africa, people were feeling the effects of COVID, but never did I hear of a lot of people feeling that they had no one that had their back. African culture is underpinned by long-term, well-established and meaningful relationships in your life. It doesn't imply that everything is always sunshine and roses for African people; it just means that you cope much better if you have a sense of support and community as a given in your life. And when you don't, it translates into a very, very scary statistic.

This concept of having ones back, and the impact it can have on an individuals' success, has also been emphasised by Keith Ferrazzi, who did a research study on "who's got your back," which resulted in a huge breakthrough, disregarding the myth of the lone professional "superman" and the rest of Western culture's go-it-alone mentality. He emphasised, as do I believe, that the real path to success in your work and in your life is through creating an inner circle of what he called "lifeline relationships"—deep, close relationships with a few key trusted individuals who will offer the encouragement, feedback and

For bonuses go to ...

generous mutual support every one of us needs to reach our full potential. I refer to this concept as a community; we all need to belong to a community.

Whether your dream is to lead a company, be a top producer in your field, overcome the self-destructive habits that hold you back, lose weight or make a difference in the larger world, we can only do that with and through other people. It is evident that behind every great leader, at the base of every great tale of success, you will find an indispensable circle of trusted advisors, mentors and colleagues. These groups come in all forms and sizes, and can be found at every level and in nearly all spheres of both professional and personal life, but what they all have in common is a unique kind of connection with each other; they collectively and essentially make up your relationship currency. These relationships are, quite literally, why some people succeed far more than others. All of these collective avenues to the same answer, meaning that "relationships are all there is," is why I thought that I could no longer wait. I had to share the message now, and not wait any longer. Every human being has the right to feel supported, to feel part of a community, part of something larger than themselves, and it starts with one authentic, meaningful relationship, built out into a connected pattern of multiple quality relationships, that support and lift each other and hold each other accountable towards achieving their greater good.

Ask yourself who has your back in life and in business right now. Think for yourself right now. Do you feel that you at least have one or two people that have your back in life or in business? I do hope it is a resounding YES!! This is really my wish for you. Because without that, life is hard! How much time have you really invested in building these relationships and the social capital to date? Now, those of you that have, you probably have spent a lot of time and effort in these relationships, and you are in the right place to learn more about how to build on this foundation that you have already started. And if you are someone that feels that maybe you don't have as many valuable relationships as you would like, then continue reading; you are also in the right company, and you will build it step by step as we move through this process together.

Good Idea, Good Partner; What Is More Important?

"If people like you, they'll listen to you; but if they trust you, they'll do business with you."
– Zig Ziglar

Based on personal experience and my own research over the last few decades, from a business perspective, through engaging with other successful business leaders, and interviewing and studying the top leaders of our century, I will share many of the insights, tips and advice I got along the way. I look forward to sharing this with you in the next chapters.

I also exchanged ideas with authors who have researched all the wealthiest families in the world, who have transferred money from one generation to another, while succeeding in being fulfilled in their extended family units. And the one common thing that they and I found irrespectively, is that all of these people have an inner circle of connected relationships. They are not people that work on their own to build a business. Even if you look at someone like Bill Gates, it looks like Bill Gates stands on his own. No, he doesn't. He has a team that has been with him from the start, and even his wife, Melinda Gates, built Microsoft with him from the start. He, too, has an inner circle of connected relationships that supported him from the start, to help build the type of business that has impacted millions, if not billions, of people in this world.

When we truly want to make a real impact at a global level, or like Elon Musk at a galactic level, we need to do it with and through other people—we do it in teams; we don't do it completely on our own. But if we don't have the trust in place, if we don't have those quality relationships in place, you won't have the confidence to share. It is about sharing.

Unfortunately, when relationships are not that well established, we can have challenges with people when we start building a business together. And when you start making money and becoming successful in your business venture, and you don't have really strong relationships, it's worse, not better, than when you are not yet making the money. Because when you start making the money in business, it magnifies the character of individuals. And that can very often cause the downfall of the business.

So, I've realised that the number one thing is to know who you are in business with, which means that you need to ask yourself all the time: "What is the quality of my relationship?" That is more important than the actual business that you are doing. If you have a good business concept, but you have the wrong partners, your business will not succeed. And if you have an average idea, but you have very good partners, you have a lot higher likelihood to succeed in business, which is not something that is often shared with aspiring leaders or when you just start your career.

Why Is the Timing Now for You?

*"If you only have a hammer,
you tend to see every problem as a nail."*
– Abraham Maslow

When deciding to share this information, I had someone in mind that is an employee aspiring to become an influential leader, or an entrepreneur that wants to start their own business—someone who wants to make money and have a good living, AND for whom just making money is no longer good enough—and wants to feel like what they are doing matters, and that they are contributing something by giving their time and talents to the world. There's nothing wrong with making a good living; in fact, I would like to encourage you to get rewarded handsomely for the real value and contribution that you make.

But there's a way in which we can make a lot of money, right? But maybe not like many people had previously done it throughout the Industrial Age, by putting themselves in the central position of importance, often at the detriment of others, and sometimes at the expense of many things, like the globe, the environment, turning a blind eye to child labor, etc. I know that if you are reading this, you want to do things differently. So, I have subsequently realised that anyone seeking to achieve something that will contribute to more people than only themselves, will most certainly find value in what you are reading.

I know that many of you have this need—yes, you want a good lifestyle—but you also want to give back; you want to do something that's important. Many of the people I have coached, students of mine, have explained to me that they are getting impatient with the old ways of how businesses run, but they don't really know exactly how to tackle it in a way that they can change it. Many of you feel disempowered; you don't know how to change it. And if you don't have influencers, like reading my book or listening to my webinars or podcasts, or attending seminars where this experience is shared with you, the only people that you can look at as a leadership example, are very often the people that are doing exactly the traditional business that you don't necessarily want to do future focused. So how do you learn? It's also about speed of execution; if you want to achieve things faster, you need to have a more powerful and a more connected relationship network of people that share your vision. Building this connected relationship is something I understand well, and this is why I want to teach you how to actually get that done in a meaningful way. What I am sharing with you is built on the fact that everything you

For bonuses go to ...

would like to achieve in life is going to be achieved through and with people, like I said to you in the beginning. If you really want to have access to resources, to knowledge and to opportunities, that's also going to happen through people. It's something that you really have to deliberately focus on. To have really extraordinary and successful relationships, you don't connect to people that are of that nature just because you are lucky or you are unusually well positioned, or there's just a great chemistry—you actually have to work at it, you have to plan, you have to be determined and deliberate, you have to apply a practice of authenticity and collaboration, and you have to build trust. So, it's on those foundations that I'm sharing with you.

As we move forward in the book, I would like to quote Wayne Dyer as a point of reflection for you: "Who do you need to become now in order to attract that which you desire? And the only thing separating you from it is time." In other words, you already know what you want to do. And you are becoming the person that would do that. But it will just take time until you get to that end goal. So who is that person that you need to become? And this is something I urge you to think about. It's not easy to answer, so you might not get the answer today, but it's a worthwhile consideration; it's an important first step to understanding why now, for you... If you need coaching support to identify and understand your big "why," go to my page at www.connectedrainmaker.com to see how you can be coached by me.

The "Haves" and the "Have Nots"

"Only a life lived for others is a life worthwhile."
– Albert Einstein

Zig Ziglar used to say you can change who you are, and where you are, and what you're doing by changing one thing, and that's what you're putting into your mind. So people that you're spending time with are a big factor of what you're putting in your mind; the conversations you're having, the recommendations that they're giving—the collaboration, or the strategy, or the lack thereof—is so valuable. Mark Timm echoed my belief that relationships are the new currency, and he said to me that he learnt that from his mentor, Kevin Harrington, the original "shark" from *Shark Tank*, as well as Zig Ziglar, who was his mentor in his young adulthood.

Not everybody can grow a business profitably and scale a business. Having relationships, having people you can call, is what is critical; we were not put on this Earth to be alone. We weren't designed to be alone. We weren't supposed to be alone. The fact that there are people out there trying to do this thing of life alone, they're asking to climb a mountain that they're not supposed to climb. And, you know, we are supposed to be in relationships, we're supposed to be in communities, we're supposed to be in masterminds, because we are supposed to help each other. Knowing we're not supposed to be alone, knowing we're not supposed to do this alone, then why are people still doing it? Why are people not raising their hand and asking for help?

If you were to research those people in the world that have mentors helping them, and those that don't—I call it "the haves and the have nots"—there are more people in the "have not" category than there are in the "haves." And the only thing that separates the "haves" and the "have nots," is some vulnerability and some authenticity to say, "I don't have it all figured out. I actually need people in my life to help me, to guide me, to coach me and to mentor me in this crazy thing called life, in love, relationships and business. And I'm willing to be coached; I'm willing to be helped." And you know this already: When the student is ready, the teacher appears.

Relationships are not just about love and the essence of kindness and having someone in your corner, but it's also about growth; massive growth in terms of getting you to think differently. Relationships or connections have the propensity to move us forward, and to move us left when we think it's right. Relationships can teach us so much about ourselves.

I started doing some research about people that have succeeded in having a fulfilled life. So let me define success. From my perspective, success has a financial component, but that's certainly not the only component. Success is also about fulfilment of self, and fulfilment in your personal life, who you are as a human being, and the impact that you have on the world. And then finances are a component of that success or fulfilment. I identified some of these successful people in Africa, Asia, America and Europe, whom I had the opportunity to interview and speak to, and I have also drawn on my own experiences and insights I have had during my rich career and life, working and travelling to over 100 different places globally. Now I feel grateful and privileged to have this opportunity to share some of these impactful and meaningful insights with you.

In the chapters moving forward, I will share with you some of the profound insights I have learnt about the power and value of authentic relationships, and I will guide you on a journey, showing you some of the foundational steps that you need to get in place if you want to see the impactful results in your life and in the lives of others that you touch. Go now to Chapter 3, where we will start exploring what drives you in life, and why you should get connected.

Chapter 3

Why Do You Want to Be Connected?

Don't Take Only My Word for It

> *"If your emotional abilities aren't in hand,*
> *if you don't have self-awareness, if you are not able*
> *to manage your distressing emotions, if you can't have*
> *empathy and have effective relationships, then no matter*
> *how smart you are, you are not going to get very far."*
> – Daniel Goleman

A respected friend and colleague of mine, who is a world-renowned psychologist, has helped many families and individuals from many different countries all over the world. She has also been the anchor psychologist for a TV series called *Saving Our Marriage*. She always says that her first and most important relationship on planet Earth is her relationship with herself, and secondly, and an equal and opposite 50%, the relationship she has with other people. One of the key elements we share in our approach to life and to business is that relationships are definitely at the foundation of the work that we do. The relationships in one's life, the ones that worked as well as the ones that didn't work, can teach you so much. Of course, we all wish to have relationships that work, and you want to have those people that are backing you up, that stand behind you, that believe in you, and that cheer you on.

For bonuses go to ...

But it's equally important to recognise those relationships that didn't work, and the relationships that equally brought you pain and challenges and obstacles; they also came to serve you greatly. They came to take you out of your comfort zone and step you into another level of being. So, you need to equally give credit to the relationships in your life that have and still work, and the relationships that didn't. This is a very important aspect about relationships: that you look at both sides. You can compare a relationship to a coin, knowing that every coin has two sides, and knowing equally that every relationship always has two sides. In a sense, it's about coming to the realisation that each relationship in our lives is a blessing, and it should not be based on expectations, but rather being focused on being grateful for the engagement. You can or will draw something of value either way, good or bad. My friend, Ilze, likes to say that the angels and the devils that came in human form, all came to serve her and to shape her. Who are some of the people that you have in your life, both good and challenging, that if you think back, brought great opportunities for learning, and gifts into your life?

Another trusted friend and colleague of mine, Frans (who was mentored by Raymond Ackerman, an esteemed businessman that has made the Forbes list of Africa's Richest many times), is an expert in retail in emerging markets, and has assisted groups like Fruit and Veg City, and Food Lovers Markets, to establish themselves on the African continent, across 11 countries. He is a successful man, no doubt, who also emphatically said, when I asked him about the importance of relationships in his business success, that it had an enormous role in his success in life and in business. In fact, he went right back to his years as a child, as he thought back to his first meaningful "business relationship" and shared with me the story about his godfather, Yanis Marais, who started the Trust Bank in South Africa, a progressive bank for its time.

Something that stood out to Frans was Yanis' commitment to service, and his focus on customer centricity, which was way ahead of its time in banks. And he reminisced about walks on the beach with his godfather, with their dogs, where Yanis would explain business to him. What still struck Frans as he spoke to me, was how his godfather had treated him like an equal, which was so wonderful to him as a school boy. To Frans, this was a serious, almost businesslike relationship that he had at that age of his life, which played such an important role moving forward in his life. It taught him that people are the most important, whichever way you do it. And whichever way you look at things, it will always come back to the people in that equation. And that's all about relationships. So to Frans, relationships have been the foundation of what he has done, and will continue to be the primary focus. Listening to Frans, I could not help thinking back about the many people that had impacted my life meaningfully, and also wondering about who I was paying this forward to in my life now. Who has impacted your life meaningfully? And have you been paying it forward?

Are You Crushing It in Business, and Being Crushed at Home?

> *"If civilization is to survive, we must cultivate the science of human relationships—the ability of all peoples, of all kinds, to live together, in the same world at peace."*
> – Franklin D. Roosevelt

Not too long ago, I had the opportunity to speak to a successful serial entrepreneur in the USA: Mark. Business comes easy to Mark, and he shared with me that at a certain point in his career, he realised that he was winning at work, but he was losing at home. He was crushing it in all of his business endeavours, and he was getting crushed at home. When I asked him if he believed that relationships are very important for one's success in life and in business, it was a big astounding yes!! He shared with me that he was sitting in his driveway

For bonuses go to ...

one day, and he literally came to a realisation: What if the most valuable business that he would ever own, ever operate or ever be part of, was the one he was going home to, not the one he went to that day?

And that's when he realized that all of these businesses that he was involved in, all of these business endeavours, were just practice—they were just practice so that he could bring home his first and his best, instead of his last and his least. It was then that he realised that the most valuable business is the one you go home to, which is family. He also shared with me that he believed that when all the chips are on the table, when we are at the end of all that we know, the only real currency that we will have at our fingertips is our relationships—the people we are meaningfully connected to. He confirmed that for him, relationships are the most valuable asset that one will ever have in their entire lifetime. And in a final pondering moment, he reflected and said: "So how important are relationships to me right now? They're probably at the very top of my list of priorities for this second phase of my life."

To be vulnerable is a critical skill in creating authentic relationships, in life and in business. I will share a story with you that was shared with me a while ago by a dynamic gentleman. For this gentleman, to be a good father was very important, and at some point, he realised that his role as businessman had really impacted his role as a present father. He then decided to make a very clear shift, and he went on to tell me that he felt very vulnerable in this process, because he felt that what he had to do was sit down and apologise to his family, for not being the father and husband that they should have had. He told me that no matter how successful he had been in business, to sit down and apologise to his wife and children was a very scary step for him, and he felt so vulnerable and weak in that moment, because he was not used to feeling so exposed.

He got a smile on his face as he was telling me that even though these were the emotions he was facing at that time, if his young adult children were to tell me about that moment right now, they would say that they had never seen their father stronger or more confident in their entire lives than they had seen him that day—taking responsibility for his mistakes, for his misgivings and for not being who they needed. And it was in fact the beginning of their relationship from that point forward.

Why am I sharing this story with you? Because, you see, if you want to have real relationships, make sure that you own your stuff; make sure you take responsibility for your stuff in that relationship. And what ended up happening for him was that he then had his family hold him accountable to be the best version of himself from that moment onwards. And what he did not realise was that this behaviour set the tone for being a role model to his children, because once his children became teenagers, guess what happened? Now when they're struggling, when they are making bad decisions, who do they come to and ask to please be held accountable to be a better version of themselves today? Their father. He did not have to fight with his kids, because he showed them what it looks like to be held accountable, so that when it was time for them to be held accountable, they chose him to hold them accountable. Think for a moment about what relationship you might not be holding yourself accountable for right now? And what are all the good things that could potentially happen if you did start doing it?

For bonuses go to ...

Lessons from the African Village

"We cannot seek achievement for ourselves and forget about progress and prosperity for our community... Our ambitions must be broad enough to include the aspirations and needs of others, for their sakes and for our own."
– Cesar Chavez

If we look at the African continent, I would like to refer back to "the African village" as context, referring to what the African village was before slavery and colonialism. It was based purely on relationships, on your connectedness with others as part of a community. The entire mechanism was about relationships; business was about relationships. And remember, Africa wasn't really—contrary to popular belief—a war-based continent; it was a peaceful continent. And it was a continent that was about trading, from the Queen of Sheba through to Mansa Musa. Relationships have been important throughout the history of Africa. This is one thing we have often missed out on in our businesses, from an African perspective, because we have disregarded the African history.

Globally, we have so often looked at the last couple of 100 years as our history as a human race. The tendency is to bring in the history of the last couple of 100 years ONLY, and it is good to learn from other context, like the west and the north; however, those essential values that were present on the African continent, where all humans essentially originate from, are never or not often enough brought into business in general. At the heart of that is the relationship. So, relationships are essentially the currency of Africa, and are becoming the currency of leadership success and business success at a global scale. For the future, if we are going to build sustainable businesses on a global scale, these values will need to be considered, and the biggest of them all is relationships. This is necessary for long-term sustainability. The relationship is going to be at the heart. This is already evident in some pockets of excellence; great companies are growing as communities in today's world—the global currency is becoming relationships.

What we often do is that we run out and want to make a quick buck. So we throw a few things together, and people see that Africa is a new market, and they might be thinking, let's go there and make money. But it won't be sustainable, and you're not going to make it in the medium to long term, because it is about the relationship. When we are prepared to go into Africa with a mindset of building relationships, then we are going to build the important, sustainable businesses that will last for another 100, 200 or 300 years, not just those in-and-out initiatives. And that is just why the relationship is so exceptionally important on the African continent. It's important everywhere, but even more so in Africa.

Have you ever seen a more genuine smile and a hug than on the African continent? And they are unconditional, mostly, because Africans exude customer centricity. It's how Africans are wired. So it's all about relationships; it is definitely the currency of Africa. If we look at the African village, remember that the African village was never about an individual; Africans have something that is referred to as the "we culture." It was always about the good of the village, and that's where the African proverb stems from: "It takes a village to raise a child." And of course, the other beautiful thing about the village, which is so beautiful to me, is the importance of the grandmother, the wisdom of the grandmother—we keep the grandmother close to us; we keep the grandmother here with us to share her wisdom with the children—and this is another beautiful African value about relationships. So we can learn a lot from Africa about relationships, which is ultimately the continent where the human race came from.

As I have shared with you, I was privileged to live in Zululand, close to one of the Zulu tribes, and my father was a friend of the chief. So as a child, I would sometimes go with him, and I would play with the other children. My father and the Induna (the Zulu word for chief) would

For bonuses go to ...

have deep conversations, and during one of these conversations, at a certain point, the Induna called us children closer to listen to a story. The chief told us to bring him a bundle of sticks, and with huge excitement and enthusiasm, we all started running around picking up sticks, and soon we had a bundle of sticks together for him. He took one, broke it and said: "Can you see how easily I could break this single stick?" And all of us, as if we were one choir, answered, "Yes, Induna, we see!" He then said, "Let's tie a few sticks together," which he quickly did with a piece of animal skin that he had close by, and again he tried to break the sticks that were all tied together. This was difficult, and he showed us that it was almost impossible to do, to break all the sticks together. And then he went on to say, "You see, children, sticks in a bundle can't be broken, but sticks taken singly can be easily broken." And the same applies to people. Alone, we are vulnerable and weak, but together in unity, we are strong. And that's the gift of understanding the currency of relationships, the currency of being connected.

The Hungry Street Man

*"The value of life is not in its duration but in its donation.
You are not important because of how long you live;
you are important because of how effectively you live."*
– Myles Munroe

Sometimes those that might socially or socio-economically be viewed as less important, can become extremely important. Never assume that one human being is more important than another. My father was my hero, and one of the foundational values in my life were laid by him, for which I am eternally grateful. I was a little girl, and my father was waiting with me in the car, for my mother; she had gone into the bank, and he had driven us there. I was sitting in the back of the vehicle. My father said to me, "Sweetheart, you'll be okay. I am just going to quickly go into that building, but you will be able to see me. Just stay in the car; I will be right back."

I happily did what he said, and I was only about four or five years old. I watched through the car window where he was going and what he was doing. There was a take-out place just in front of the car; I think it was a Kentucky Fried Chicken or something like that. He walked in, and he purchased some food and something to drink, and then he walked out with the packet of goodies. There was a gentleman sitting on the sidewalk, a street person. And I saw my father have a conversation with him, and he gave him the parcel and came back to the car thereafter. Having the enquiring mind that I do, I hardly gave him time to get into the car, and I started asking questions. "Why did you do that, Daddy? Who is the man, Daddy? Do you know him, Daddy?" The questions came out like a floodgate had just opened up. He responded with a smile on his face, and he said to me that he did that because he knew that the man needed his help, and that he was in the privileged position of being able to get the man something to eat and drink. He said to me that I would also still meet people on my life path, whom I will know I need to help. And he said, "Today, I knew that I had the voice inside of me, telling me that I had to help him."

My father looked at me, smiled and said, "My first born, you might not understand it at this stage of your life, but I do think it's something that you need to start thinking about. You can never be too young to think about this...I want you to think about how you are going to treat other people. You have a choice to treat people respectfully or not." He said, "Whatever your choice, I will respect it, but my advice is that you should make your choice and then treat all people the same way. The important thing is that you need to be consistent. It doesn't matter who you're speaking to, or where they come from, the way in which you engage them needs to be consistent."

Today, I thank him for that advice. That piece of advice moulded, to a large extent, who I became as a person, because I made my choice to

For bonuses go to ...

respect every human being. I don't get it right 100% of the time, but I aspire to getting it right 100%. As a result, I have had such significant surprises and gifts in my life, which have brought great richness to me. I will give you the same opportunity that my dad gave me, and I will ask you: Do you know how you want to lead from where you stand? Do you know how you want to be remembered by other people? This decision is a serious decision. You see, every choice comes with responsibility and accountability, and you can only make the choice for yourself. It brings no guarantees that other people will make the same choice towards you. I want to invite you to think, and be honest with yourself: Why are you interested in knowing more about relationships and connections? Who do you want to be in those connections, and what will you stand for? What will be your legacy as you build your connector currency? There is no right or wrong answer; there is only a truthful and a less truthful answer—but the truthful answer is going to bring you greater fulfilment in your journey, so please value yourself enough to think about what the answers are to these questions for you.

Are You Careful, Careless or Caring?

"Sincerity makes the very least person to be of more value than the most talented hypocrite."
– Charles Spurgeon

There are three ways to be in a relationship, and if one understands these fundamentals, they will understand why being connected through authentic relationships is the real leadership currency.

You can choose to be careless in relationships. You can put yourself above another human being and look down on that person. When you do that, you become more careless in that relationship. Because you care less about your impact and influence on this person, you look down on them. The opposite is true if you put somebody on a pedestal, and you look up to the person. You can easily become more careful because you possibly feel a little bit intimidated, thinking you are not on their level, and in a sense, walking on eggshells. In this instance, you become careful in relationships. A true, authentic relationship—and this is what we should strive for in our own relationships—should be caring, and this can only be achieved when we regard each other as equals in our sharing and connection.

I strive to help my clients and the people that I coach and mentor, to understand that we are equals. And when you perceive yourself as an equal to any other human being, it doesn't matter the age, the sex or the race; you become caring, and a caring relationship brings the biggest return on investment (ROI), and the greatest fulfilment. A careless and a careful relationship will not bring that to you. Please go to www.connectedrainmaker.com if you want to learn more about how you can be coached by me.

If we start with the self, when we start by first looking into ourselves, before we start judging or blaming or being angry with others, I think this will take us a long way forward in terms of fulfilled relationships, and fulfilled means getting something of value. So, you cannot always control if that person will be amenable to you or not. But nevertheless, you still have the choice to take that as a rich experience. If your approach is to evaluate if it goes well or proverbially good or bad, that is irrelevant, because it's actually neutral; but if you approach it as an opportunity to harvest the pearls of wisdom or the richness that it provides from the experience, you grow as an individual.

Your relationships with others are simply mirrors of your relationship with yourself. People treat you exactly the way you unconsciously treat yourself. Their outer mannerisms toward you reflect your inner mannerisms, so one of the most powerful ways to transform your life is to become consciously aware of your beliefs and feelings about yourself. The ones who push your buttons the most are your greatest teachers. If you can bring your lopsided perceptions back into balance,

For bonuses go to ...

you'll appreciate them as your teacher; if you can't, you'll blame them for being a button pusher. As you grow in wisdom, you'll learn to embrace and love others for who they are, looking for the benefits they offer you, and knowing that they represent parts of you that you've buried or disowned. Wisdom means thanking others for bringing to your awareness those areas where you have lied to yourself and not loved yourself, and for being grateful that they've given you this opportunity to love not only others but also yourself.

What I have learnt is that we will also have ad hoc engagements with people that will come into our lives and leave again. This is the way of the universe to assist us in being exposed to both sides of love: support and challenge. We often don't realise that it's the challenging people in our lives, working hand in hand with the supportive ones, who help us to get where we are going in life. We need the balance of support and challenge, of positive and negative feedback, to grow and evolve. The degree to which we appreciate both sides and embrace life is the degree to which we become enlightened.

Have Everything in Life You Want

*"You can have everything in life you want,
if you will just help other people get what they want."*
– Zig Ziglar

Whatever you focus on becomes your reality. When you focus on the lack in your relationships, that becomes your reality. When you start focusing on the richness and the good in your relationships, that becomes your reality. So be reminded that your focus becomes your reality. Focus on what you wish to be your reality.

Dr. William Danko, author of *The Millionaire Next Door*, has done over 30 years of research on the wealthy people in the USA, and has drawn incredible wisdom around how people should create prosperity. When

www.connectedrainmaker.com

I had the privilege of engaging and speaking to him over the Christmas period in 2020, he said to me that from his perspective, relationships are his life, and he shared countless examples of how relationships shaped his world since he was a young academic researcher. He also highlighted that along with relationships, one should remember that the harder we work, the luckier we get, and he drew on one of the baseball analogies, and said that you can't get a home run unless you get up to bat, and what he meant is that you have to lead with giving, in order to get—it's about thinking of the collective, and that is what ultimately will bring the fulfilment.

You can have everything in life you want, if you will just help enough other people get what they want. Now, what are you in control of in that statement? The word "enough?" The question really is, how many people do you want to serve? How many people do you want to help? The renowned futurist and entrepreneur, Peter Diamandis, said: "If you want to become a billionaire, help a billion people." The point is that so many times, we make things too hard. And what we really need to focus on is helping other people be abundant, or thinking and solving problems for other people. We don't have to sell anybody anything. We just have to solve a problem they have. And when we do that, when we help enough people, then what we most desire will come to pass. And so that's really the wisdom. We're all in the helping business; we are all connected. We're in the serving business, and if you truly help enough people, you won't have to want for anything in your life again.

Byron Tully, who has been researching and writing about the core values that people who've had wealth for three generations or more end up adopting, and how these families maintain their financial security, their quality of life and their commitment to their community, has in a recent discussion with me shared that one of the Indian businessmen that he interviewed in his research endeavours about generational wealth, said to him that if you want to be wealthy, you need to recognise God within you, and you need to "just be a little

For bonuses go to www.connectedrainmaker.com

piece of God on Earth." And what I think he was trying to say within his context, is to not only be of service to others, but to be of service to others based on what they need, and based on what you have to give from inside yourself, and when those different aspects meet, it's the winning recipe, and everyone wins. Take the time to really listen to your inner calling. Take the time to really listen to what it is that you are meant to do. If you take that time, it will be paid back to you in dividends of fulfilment that I cannot describe. We will take a look at how you get to know your inner calling, later on in the book, but let's first get to the next chapter, which will shed light on how to get your core community together, your "power of 5."

Chapter 4

The Average of 5

If You Wanna Get Sick, Hang Out with Sick People

"In the company of the good, we become good."
— Dutch Proverb

You have probably heard people say that you become the average of the 5 people you spend the most time with, and some people even say that today in business and in life, being connected is the real leadership currency. The motivational speaker Jim Rohn famously said that we are the average of the five people we spend the most time with. This relates to the law of averages, which is the theory that says the result of any given situation will be the average of all outcomes. When we think of this in relationship or connected terms, we are greatly influenced, consciously or unconsciously, by the people that are closest to us. It affects our way of thinking, our self-esteem and our decisions. We remain our own person, but some research has shown that we are more affected by our environment than we think. There's also the derivative to the above that says, "Show me your friends and I'll show you your future."

The whole premise of how this came to be was interesting to me, and so I ventured out to have discussions with some successful people internationally. I did some research and also drew on my own

For bonuses go to ...

experiences to understand more about the legitimacy or the general perspective regarding the power of five. When embarking on this research process, I had to stop and smile at the conundrum of the situation, because part of the process to reach some of my conclusions were exactly that; I was drawing on mentors, and people in my network that have the qualities of success and fulfilment in their lives. And one of the first masterpieces I was reminded of during my search, was the famous quote of Sir Isaac Newton, who said: "If I have seen further, it is by standing on the shoulders of giants."

"Standing on the shoulders of giants" is a metaphor that means, "Using the understanding gained by major thinkers who have gone before, in order to make progress." You see, when you surround yourself with the people that are aligned with what you are striving to achieve in your life—when they speak the language that you speak, meaning a way of being, feeling or a way of thinking, the language of your mind or your heart—it changes everything. When you surround yourself on that sphere of influence and awareness of people equal or greater than you, you can grow to your next level. So early on, I already confirmed that one's personal relationships are incredibly important.

An influencer went further to say that if you want to get sick, hang around sick people, and if you want to lift yourself up, you lift yourself up with a board—a personal board of directors, so to speak. The quality of the relationships we surround ourselves with, have a significant impact on how we express ourselves, conduct ourselves and who we become as a human. This gentleman shared a story with me about a colleague of his, whom he referred to as Dr. Denise, which I want to share with you. As a young lady, Dr. Denise was told by the people around her to go to college and to get a secure job, and there is nothing wrong with that in principle, but what those advising her did not realise was that as a young lady, this advice (although well intentioned) limited her thinking of what would be possible for her in life; until thankfully, one of her science teachers in college told Denise that she could have higher aspirations, and that she could become a physician. This one conversation had such a profound impact on Denise that she went on to be a radiologist.

This was the result of one person, a professor, taking the time to be a mentor to her, and even though nobody else was telling her that, she was surrounded by her teacher, whom she trusted and could show her the way. You see, you never know how far the impact could spread, from the advice of one person, a mentor, and in Dr. Denise's case, not only did it impact her life, but she took it a step further. She has a son, and it was important for her to be a role model to him, so she opened up a radiology clinic in a poor section of town, for underserved communities, and today she serves and impacts many people's lives as a result. Not only has her life been impacted, but she went on to do something exceptional, which is now changing and impacting many people's lives as a result of the centre that she created. Through that one person who encouraged her to be more than what she thought she could be, because they saw that gift in her, she went on to impact multiple lives. Do you have a mentor or coach in your life as part of your care team? I help many people like you through my mentoring and coaching programmes, and if you think this is something that you would like to learn more about, please go to www.connectedrainmaker.com and see how you can be supported by me.

By Design, or Consequential

"People may hear your words, but they feel your attitude."
– John C. Maxwell

The influence that people around you have is tremendous. Some people say it starts with the influences you get from your family, then possibly one or two very influential and inspirational teachers, coaches or mentors, and then the person you marry. What most successful

For bonuses go to ...

people have in common is that they believe it is critically important for us to have a coach at all times in our lives, whom we feel connected to, and whom has achieved what we would like to achieve, so that we can learn from their experience. We don't have to learn everything the hard way. If we want to make a larger impact, we want to learn the fast-track way, by learning from other people's experiences and building on that, so that you are able to offer what you foster with your coach, plus what you've added to that, to the next generations. It thus enriches continuously into the next generations. One should reach for a quality of life, rather than a standard of living. Have you heard the old saying that when you don't have any money, you're going to know who your friends are, and when you have money, your friends are going to know who you are?

One of the beautiful things about relationships is to empower the other person to hold you accountable. The proverbial average of the five is impacted by how much power you give them to hold you accountable and to lovingly be a mirror to you. A beautiful story that was shared with me was about a father and his children. You see, he wanted to be a better dad, and one of the things that he was mad at himself about was that he would sometimes take his phone with him when he put the kids to bed. And he would look at the phone instead of being present with them while putting them to bed. He really wanted to be a better father and have a stronger relationship with his children. So what he did was that he asked his kids to hold him accountable the next time he brought his phone out when putting them to bed; they would have the authority to take it from him and remove it from the room.

Inevitably, at some point, it did happen; in fact, he told me that it still happened dozens of times before he broke his habit. And every time, he was embarrassed and disappointed in himself. But over time, he learned to be present with his kids, but only because they held him accountable to be present with them, because he had asked them to hold him accountable. So be mindful that it is one thing to merely have a relationship, but it's a whole other thing to have relationships where you can ask the other person to hold you accountable to be the best version of yourself. When considering the five people around you, do your best to surround yourself with people that aren't afraid, and are empowered, to hold you accountable when you are not the best version of yourself.

A friend of mine worked with what he referred to as "a lot of damaged people," and he clarified that by saying "people that are quite violent, and often in prison." A specific example he drew on was a group of 12 pedophiles in a prison, that he had to go work with over a period of nine months. He shared that as a father himself, when he first arrived there, he thought a little differently about how he wanted to respond. And over time, he truly got to understand them and the situations that got them to this point in their lives, and he did this primarily through listening. When I asked him about his perspective on "the power of 5" concept, I was not surprised to hear a slight variation in response. He said to me: "You know, Ezanne, I'm more inclined to hang out with fellow freaks; you know I've never enjoyed hanging around with people who think the same way I do. I don't think there are evil people; I really don't. I don't think anyone wakes up in the morning and says they may be terrible, but I think there are people that have influenced our lives, whom we have to either simulate or understand what that means to us."

It's certainly an interesting perspective. So I referred back to the prisoners and asked him how they would fit into this discussion. He explained to me that he did not think he would ever let those people influence his life, but that he thought he could choose or decide how people impacted his life. He said that if you're not doing it by design, it's then consequential. And if it's consequential, then you become very definitely like those that are around you. Because you're not analyzing it, you're not being objective about whether it's good or bad, or both. His perspective gave me insight as to why building authentic relationships by design has been such a rewarding experience for me

For bonuses go to ...

and other successful people, and why I wanted you to know how to do it too. How have you chosen your close relationships to date—consequentially or by design?

The Wisdom of the Ancient Greeks

> *"Every successful individual knows that his or her achievement depends on a community of persons working together."*
> – Paul Ryan

The ancient Greeks had so many words for love, whereas in English, we have one word for love: we "love" rugby, especially if you are from South Africa. We "love" what we call "braaivleis," which is BBQ; we "love" the sunshine; we "love" our family; we "love" chocolate...you see, it is difficult to identify distinction in the word. Yet the ancient Greeks had many words for love, right? They used the word "Philia" to describe your love for a brother, a sister and a close friend, and then the word for erotic or romantic love is "Eros," and unconditional love is "Agape." And even the love for your mother-in-law has a specific category, which is "Storge," and these are different concepts.

The ancient Greeks also brought us the concept of time. With the concept of time, there was the same distinction in the ancient Greek language. Again, in English, we have one word, "time." The ancient Greeks had three beautiful connotations. The first was "Cronos," from which we derived the concept of chronological time; in other words, the time on your watch. With Cronos, every second is just like every other second; there are 60 seconds in a minute and 60 minutes in an hour. The second concept was called "Kairos," lesser known but no less important. And Kairos was described as appropriate time; the dictionary definition is a time when conditions are right for the accomplishment of a crucial action, the opportune and decisive moment. And from a more philosophical perspective, it would refer to the concept of "deep time"—you know, when the world seems to stop entirely.

Richard Rohr refers to Kairos as those moments in life where you stop and say, "This is as perfect as it can be." Or, "It doesn't get any better than this." We all know those moments, don't we? They may be few and far between, but sometimes a Kairos moment in life can feed your soul, like fuel, for many months at a time. There is an element of serendipity, and a feeling of ceasing an opportunity, in those precious moments where time stands still and everything feels possible. It is where the minute stops, and it becomes a moment that lasts for eons. When you find yourself in Kairos time, you completely lose track of Cronos time. A state of flow is activated, and it cannot be measured but only experienced. There is also a third concept of time one can consider, which are broad sweeps of time, such as millennia, generations and decades.

When it comes to thinking through the quality of your connection, the significant relationships, you think about the Kairos moments that you have shared together. It means we can relive them even 20 years down the line. It's about what we are doing in the moment. How are we relating to that person? Connected relationships are about how we relate; the significance lies in the moment. So when looking at the quality of our connections (relationships), there is a kind of a mathematical formula, which we know is never an exact science, but it helps me to think through my own balance, what the thing is that I'm bringing, and I also think about the people I could find right now and say, "Remember what we talked about 20 years ago, or remember that amazing place where we had a dinner together, or watched a sunset, or that walk we did together in the bushveld, or when we graduated together?" And that's when that relationship means I will drop almost everything to listen, and maybe be helpful. Let's have a closer look at this mathematical formula in connections.

For bonuses go to ...

The Simple Maths of Connections

> *"Choose to focus your time, energy and conversation around people who inspire you, support you and help you to grow into your happiest, strongest, wisest self."*
> – Karen Salmansohn

For me, what a quality relationship means is that there's mutual care. There's mutual value, there's authenticity and a strong trust base, linked with love. I think we can love every other human being that we engage. And I have people across the world that I can say are quality relationships, but it does not mean that I see them on a regular basis, due to geographical constraints. But I have no doubt in my mind that the connections I have with those people are quality connections. But how do I know the difference between a quality and a quantity connection (relationship)?

Energy is absolutely critical in any relationship. So what do I mean by energy? Energy contributes significantly in terms of how we engage from a relational perspective. We can have relationships that drain our energy; we can have positive relationships that really spark and spiral up our energy. What's always helped me to think through the quality of my relationships is to apply some very simple mathematics. Good friends of mine, Colin and Steve, shared this concept with me around simple maths, and I have used it ever since.

How does it work? Well, we have addition, so we have adders of energy in our life. And there are people that we can think of right now that we could write the name down and just draw a nice big smiley face next to their name. These smiley faces add energy to me. Similarly, the reality in our world is that sometimes we have people in our lives who subtract for whatever reason, but it doesn't make them good people or bad people. But the energy flow between us just means I'd rather not pick up the phone, or answer the doorbell, and

I'd rather not go and visit them; or I'll put off that meeting—it's just an energy issue, so it subtracts. You and I know that we don't only live in a linear world; there is also an exponential world that we can co-exist in, and in this world we can have multipliers. And so, in a linear world, it's a bit of an addition and a bit of subtraction.

But we know we live in an exponential world. We also have multipliers, and the difference to that face is that you draw the smiley face with a nice, big, healthy set of ears. Because they really listen to us, and they multiply energy by their ability to listen. Being present is also about listening—really listening to someone. When you listen from a position of being present, the explicit as well as the intrinsic value, you really start to understand a lot more about people. It's very difficult to build relationships if we're in a position of judgment, because we actually put the barrier there. In every environment, and particularly in many of the organisations where I have consulted, we have people around us that for some reason divide our energy. So, simple mathematics allows me to say, more or less, where I see the quality of my relationships with a particular individual. Are there enough people that are adding and multiplying in my life? Are there some that are subtracting and dividing? Where would I like to choose to spend more of my time? From a mapping out point of view, it has always been helpful to consider the quality of the connection. Am I drawing on that quality? You can go to www.connectedrainmaker.com to download an A4 full-size, print-ready worksheet to draw out your Connector Energy Map.

And then, of course, you have to look at the other side of the coin. What is the face that I'm bringing to the people I connect with? What is it that I'm bringing to my children after a long day online, after a long day of meetings—do I subtract? Do I multiply by my ability to listen, or do I add by spending a few minutes in the garden with a loved one, or listening to how my wife or husband's day went? This is a simple mathematical process that you can use to help you identify the quality of your connections. Start thinking about what the things are that play a role in energy. Where does it come from? How do you lose energy, and how do you gain it back again?

Why do you think energy plays such a fundamental role in outcomes, meaning being able to get your job done, or building your business, being a good parent or life partner, or achieving the goals you want? Where does energy come from? And how do we master it?

The Train to Collective Genius

*"Coming together is a beginning;
keeping together is progress; working together is success."*
– Edward Everett Hale

A friend and colleague of mine, Rija, who has also been featured in the 30th Pearl Anniversary Edition of "Who's Who in the World," and who was mentored by Peter Drucker himself, says that in business, the first question is always: "Who do you have with you?" It's not about what you know; it's about who you have with you. Who will go with you on this journey? It's not about what you will bring on this journey. No, it's who we have with us on the journey. On the journey, it is also very possible that some people may join you along the way, and other people may leave. You can think of the journey as a train ride: You are on the train, and some people will climb on the train with you, and others will leave the train, because there will be many stations on this route. Sometimes you may even be the one who will choose to leave the train.

Wherever you are, you will find people who resonate at the same level as you. If you decide to follow me, or if you register for my coaching programs, and you really take it seriously, you will really improve yourself and, at the same time, you can expect that some of your friends will laugh at you, and will possibly even make fun of you—just get ready for it. But on the other side of the coin, the positive side of that coin, is that new people who are moving forward will get attracted to you. You don't have to get rid of the old friends, because the new friends will come in that you'll want to spend time with. And the old friends that no longer resonate, will wither away on their own. Often, during this journey, you will need to reflect, and the question will be "who will influence who?"

We are not static beings. We are evolving beings on this journey. People come into our lives for different reasons in different seasons—sometimes for convenience, sometimes because of where our mindset is, and sometimes because of where we spend our time. The process starts with you. Three things will happen on your journey. And I would want to have someone with me on that journey, who would help me with those three things. The three things are: LEARN, RELEARN and OPTIMISE THROUGH GROWTH. You might ask, why learning? Well, you don't know everything, so you need to discover new things on that journey, things you have never experienced before. It's about exploring the unknown—it's future focused.

But there is also another element to consider: unlearning. There are many things you need to forget, and you need to have people with you in your connections to help you to unlearn, to selectively forget the things that may hamper your present and can block your future—this is about reworking the past. And then there will be people on your journey that will help you to optimise your present. You know, as a leader, as an entrepreneur, as a business owner, you have two main challenges—to deliver today and to create tomorrow—and you need a team to help you deliver on both. The environment is changing rapidly, and it's not going to be reversible. The greatest danger in times of turbulence is not the turbulence. The greatest danger is to act with yesterday's logic. That's the greatest danger, to act with yesterday's logic. So this is why, in the relationships you have, you would want your crew, your team, to help you to optimise the present and create the future.

For bonuses go to ...

Research shows that groups, teams or the crew fall apart at 150 people. So you can't manage a lot of connections; the power of five is your circle around you, and those are considered strong links. The problem with that is, they know everybody that you know. So, when you lose a job, you need to find funding, or many other things; you're stuck. You need to expand your group beyond the "power of 5," to 25 or 50 people, and they will get you anything or anywhere that you want, so this would be the diversified quality connections. Linda Hill, an economist from Harvard Business School, when addressing a group of business people in Boston, said: "Remember, business is not a solo genius. Business is a collective genius. And the question is, who do you have with you?" To use Linda's words, what we are exploring together is the magic formula that creates that collective genius.

The Two-Stick Dance, Quality and Quantity

"Individually, we are one drop. Together, we are an ocean."
– Ryunosuke Satoro

Although every person I spoke to supported the notion that we are influenced by the people closest to us, the notion of specifically five did not deliver consensus. Five is a finite number, and it assumes that five is all we can manage, and some people I have spoken to believe that this might not be the case. The notion was shared that we are like an elastic band; we can stretch a little more in terms of who we invite in, who we include in our relationships, and build the quantity so that it's a mixture of quantity and quality—a blend—which I have coined as the "relationship mix."

In fact, some thought leaders have even proposed that especially within the context of social media, and our huge rate of participation with people that we possibly have never even met in person before, the consideration now becomes that we are possibly not the average of the five people we surround ourselves with. It is probably way bigger, and we are possibly the average of all the people we are surrounded with. Take a look around you and make sure you are in the right surroundings, in alignment with who you want to be and what you want to stand for. It is almost like a general audit of the people around you from time to time, and making sure that you are spending time with the people who are in line with what you want for your own life, and how you want to bring meaning to other people's lives.

It reminds me of the Zulu saying: "We are fighting with two sticks." And it stems from the ancient art of stick fighting. The martial art of stick fighting, which young Zulu boys grow up with, is the ability to defend and attack because they have two sticks. And if one stick is broken or gets hit away, they are very vulnerable and open to attack with only the one stick. It's almost like an extraordinary dance in terms of how they fight with these two sticks, using one foot for defense and one for attack. We need two sticks as we build our connections, because that's what's going to give us the armour against uncertainty and an uncertain future; not specifically as a defense and attack, but rather as a blend of quality and quantity. There's a beautiful African proverb that says, "If you want to go fast, go alone. But if you want to go far, go together." We can do stuff on our own, and we can start a quick business, and we can go fast. But if we want to go far, we need the people around us, we need the communities, we need the trust, we need the buy-in, and we need the purpose and the why. Most certainly, if you want to go far, go together.

There is an indigenous tribe in the Amazon that has a group of people who are currently singing a song, better known as 'the song that never ends'. The legend goes that this song started many, many years ago. Women picked up the sound of the wind and storm, as they were doing their chores, carrying water from the river to their village, washing clothes and many other tasks, they started mimicking the sounds of nature. Over time the sounds became a type of synchronised singing, and even evolved into lyrics, that resulted into a song. The legend has it that as some of the women left, others arrived and picked up the singing and continued on, and at night the men would take over some of the signing until the women took over again in the morning. The song never stops being sung...this song still continues to be sung today, as legend has it, this has been going on over centuries.

This is such a great metaphor for how we go about building authentic, interconnected relationship. It is like this song that's being sung since the beginning of time. If it evolves authentically, it is always greater than any one single person in the community. There never is an 'end state". Building a network of relationships is not about one single moment, it's a process, a fluid process that requires quality or Kairos moments, combined with quantity. It is never perfect, it is always evolving, and the continued authenticity, vulnerability, trust, love and generosity that we bring to these relationships, are similar to the way in which the men and women relieve each other throughout the day and night to keep the "song that never ends", going. This is a means to a richer experience for everyone that is part of the connection, or the network.

If you need to consider quality and quantity in relationships, how do you go about it? Where do you focus first or the most? In the next chapter, we are going to look at how we build quality and quantity in our connections.

Chapter 5

Quality, Quantity or Both?

Understanding My Relationship Mix

"Energy begets energy."
— Dolly Parton

As I have mentioned, energy is absolutely vital to our relationships. I would like to share a simple analogy with you. Let's say you take $150,000 and you buy a beautiful, luxury vehicle. It's got all the right credentials, it's got the right steering column, it's got double glazing on the windows and it's got a wonderful onboard computer. It's got a fantastic set of ABS brakes, good tires, upholstery and a fantastic sound system. At $150,000, the vehicle you are driving is sheer driving pleasure. And if the $200 battery of this amazing vehicle is flat or faulty, that vehicle is useless. Now if we look at this in human terms, we could have 30 years of business experience, we could be worth potentially millions on a salary slip and we could have many degrees and diplomas. But if my battery's flat, I just don't use those things. It takes energy to build relationships. And a fundamental principle of everything in life is that I just can't give what I don't have; do you agree? In money terms, if I don't have money, I can't give the next guy money. If I don't have it, I can't give it. If I don't have time for my children, I can't give them time. If I don't have compassion, I can't give compassion. If I don't have

For bonuses go to ...

hope, I can't give hope. And the same is true of energy. If I don't have energy in my battery, I can't help you charge yours.

You need to look after your battery; charge your battery. There are three main ways I would like to recommend that might help you do that. The first one is, find a little more balance. That in itself is an enigma; it's difficult, and you never get it completely right anyway. Even the concept of balance does not look the same from one person to another—some people love walking in nature; someone else would rather be on a quiet beach, while another person might want to read books, and others want to write. But a balance is a key thing to our energy. If I'm out of balance, my energy goes down. If I'm in balance a little more, especially in my relationships, then my energy goes up.

The second key source of energy is in our authentic relationships. This process starts with my relationship with myself. A friend of mine, Brett, likes to say that when you have a hammer in your hand, everything looks like a nail. In order to have a relationship with anyone else, you need to start by having one with yourself. Equally important are your relationships with others. It's the people I can talk to on WhatsApp or Messenger, and the people I can call for coffee. It's the people I can get into a business ventures with full trust, and this is about quality.

Third is the area of belonging; as I have said before, we were not born to be in this world alone, which relates to the quantity. What is it that we belong to? Who is it that we belong to? What is the sense of purpose that we belong to? And when I know that, I get a charge in my own energy.

It does not necessarily have to take long to build good relationships, because it is about mutual respect, and it's about understanding how to build authentic relationships. People sense respect; they sense that you are genuine about what you want to do. And if you really want their involvement, in other words, you seek collaboration. Once you have collaboration, it then becomes about continuous listening, building trust and showing respect, and then you can build those relationships fairly quickly. We have to consider that we can't get to everybody. So quality is the starting point; that's what we want to do. We want to build quality relationships, those sustainable relationships for the long-term. Still, we have to reach people—once we've listened, once we've built some relationships—and you can't do without reaching many people in today's market. I would start with the quality to gain good understanding, and once I've got the understanding, I can then do quantity. And I can then put it out on social media, to get my message across, because for many businesses, especially retail, you need volume and you need people.

So it's absolutely necessary as a next step to quantify those relationships. But you cannot do quantity if you haven't started with quality, because you need a good foundation. Once you've built the foundation on the quality, you can then use the quantity to reach more people. But always bring yourself back to the quality. Quality should be at the essence of everything: the quality relationships, the quality that you offer, the quality customer centricity; it all should be about quality because giving people quality is respect. And again, respect is at the essence of relationships.

An example is when a big international brand moved into Nigeria, and never listened to a soul. They just opened businesses, and they closed down six months later. Afterwards, they said that Nigeria is too difficult to do business with, and that you can't do business there and nobody will be able to survive, but they missed the point. They never built any relationships. Had they listened, they would have known to offer goods that were suitable for the Nigerian winter climate, but there was absolutely no relationship building. They started with the quantity, and they missed the point, because they never looked at building any quality. So in looking at this dynamic concept called a relationship, I realised that it was not about singularly identifying quantity or quality as the driver of my relationship currency, but rather the art of blending the two in an innovative and authentic relationship mix of both quality and quantity.

The Art of Relationships

> *"The purpose of relationships is to help awaken you to the inherent balance existing within and around you, and to assist you in acknowledging your own magnificence and wholeness."*
> – John F. Demartini

The art of relationship works like this, that every human being on this planet, no matter who they are, where they live or what their age is, has their own unique hierarchy of what is of highest importance, highest priority and highest value to them. And what makes you absolutely unique is this hierarchy of values.

When you ask the questions—what is this person's life showing? What is of highest importance, or highest priority? What do they spend most of their time on? What do they love to speak about? What is their focus or what are they disciplined about? What is it that I can see that energizes them? And what are they surrounding themselves with?— and when you can identify that in a person, you will understand what makes them engaged or disengaged with your invitation to connect.

For example, let's say physical exercise is important to a person that you want to make a connection with. If you want to come closer to the person—it doesn't matter who the person is—when you become critical and dismissive of physical exercise, you push the person away, and the person will pull away from you. And in between, there will be this contaminated space. But if you'll respectfully and caringly—even if it is not something that's really of importance to you—acknowledge the importance for this other person, the person will pull you closer and pull closer to you. That is the art of relationship.

In the same way, if you are an employer and you want to get more engagement from your employees, you will do your best to master this art. For example, if you want to improve your relationship with your employees, and you know what is of highest importance to them—let's say most of your team are women with smaller children—you could meet what is of highest importance to them, by giving them the opportunity to work on a flexi-time working schedule, so that they could have time in the mornings to get their children to school, and possibly pick them up again after school; they would still work the required eight hours, but it could be flexi. So now you are giving them what is important to them, and they in return would give you what is of importance to you—making sure the work is done on time. That is the art of a caring relationship.

When you want to engage in a caring relationship, truly embrace the whole person. Each person expresses love and care through their own values. Whenever something supports your values, you take away the rules. When something challenges your values, you set rules. In caring relationships, you need to think of both sides simultaneously, expressing your love for yourself and for the other person. The definition of caring is knowing someone well enough to know their values, and caring enough to express your values in terms of theirs. Read the last sentence again, and reflect on it; if you really get the deeper meaning, it's a gem to building authentic connections.

What Does Your Vesica Piscis Tell You?

"I think a winner has to be a master of preparation, they have to be a master of connection, and have really high standards for themselves and the people around them."
– Maya Moore

We naturally surround ourselves with people that are like minded to us. For instance, if you are a golfer, you're probably going to meet most

For bonuses go to ...

of your friends on the golf course. Have realistic expectations of what kind of people you want to attract in your life and have in your life. If you love drinking great wine, and you belong to a wine club, you are most likely going to meet people there that you are going to form a friendship with, or that might become more significant in your life. We form relationships with people that we feel an attraction to, and that we feel we have something in common with and share something with.

Let us look at this from a different perspective. Think of two circles that are overlapping. The name of the area of two intercepting circles is called the "vesica piscis," which is a Latin word (see the diagram below). A classic vesica piscis is formed by two overlapping circles with the same radius. The resulting shared area of the circles is an almond or fish shape. Vesica piscis is Latin for "bladder of a fish." The vesica piscis is perfectly proportioned and represents equal balance in the relationship of two circles. Equal balance is something we often strive for in our relationships and lives. It sounds ideal, but as with any ideal, equal proportion isn't always desirable or how things work out in practice. Oftentimes, there is too much or not enough overlap in our dynamic with someone or something. Have you ever wanted more of someone's attention than you're getting? Or conversely, have you felt smothered or overtaken by someone or something, such as your job for instance? Sometimes the level of intersection we desire is changeable—today we want more, tomorrow we're ready for some space. In a relationship with anything or anyone, the degree of relational overlap is fluid.

www.connectedrainmaker.com

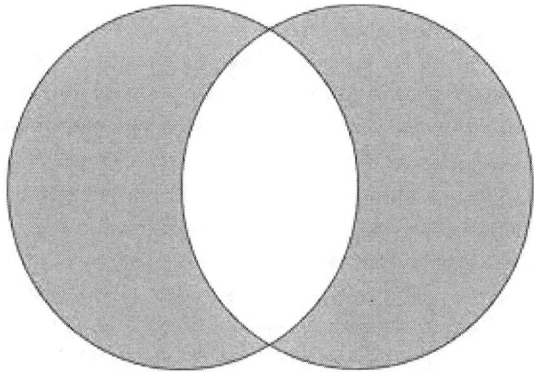

By using the vesica piscis, you can gain some insight into the dynamics of your relationships. Think of each circle of the vesica piscis as representing two entities—yourself and some "other" (a partner, child, parent, friend, your work, a hobby, and so on). Imagine yourself as one of the circles, and your "other" as the second. Draw a picture of the two circles that reflects the relationship as it is right now.

- Do the circles touch?
- Intersect a little bit?
- Practically cover over each other?
- Evaluate the dynamic of the overlap.
- Is it ideal?
- Is it the balance you want, even if it isn't equal?
- Does the overlap seem too small, leaving you feeling a bit deprived? Is it too large, making you desire a little more breathing room?

You see, the common area between the two of us, becomes the magnetic force in the relationship that pulls us together. Take the time to think about your most significant relationships, the easy ones and the difficult ones, and apply the vesica piscis principle to them—this will offer you a lot of insight on how to bring value and caring to these relationships.

For bonuses go to ...

The Power of a Greeting

> *"What I've realized is that the joy of meeting
> and greeting people from all around the world is universal."*
> – Joe Gebbia

A friend of mine, Steve, shared a story with me about the impact that a sincere greeting had on him in his early 20s when he was travelling in India. The greeting he learned is a Hindi greeting, and it is "Namaste." And what he learned is that it means that *"the divine light in me, sees or acknowledges the divine light in you."* There is something unique, special or never to be repeated when you take the time to acknowledge the presence of somebody along your journey. And what he noticed is that when people stopped to greet, they actually *stopped* to greet; they never walked past each other. During the greeting, they made a slight bow and a hand gesture.

And he learned that the bringing together of the five fingers was symbolic of the bringing together of the five senses in the greeting. And it struck him that the next thing that seemed to happen when people greeted in such a fashion, when they really acknowledged the presence of somebody along the journey, was that it opened the door for conversations. So never underestimate the power of a fully present greeting; it opens the door to conversation. And of course, when we have a series of conversations, the outcome is a relationship. We develop relationship through the conversations that we have.

As I thought about this story, I realised that Namaste has such significance, but that it is not unique in its significance, because in most of the languages in Sub-Saharan Africa, we have a very similar context to the greeting. In Zulu, when you greet someone, you would say "Sanibonani," which means *"I see you."* Taken more literally, what we are saying is that *if I see you, I have to see you; I can't look at my watch or look at my cell phone, or look at the sky as I walk past you— I must acknowledge your presence in the greeting.* In Setswana, a

Bantu language spoken in Lesotho, there is a question in the greeting, called "Dumelang," or translated means, "*Where are you?*" And the response is "Ke Teng," which means, "*I am here; I am present.*" Therefore, if I see you and we are present together, we can have a conversation. And the minute we have conversations, we can of course develop a relationship. So, the starting point of a connection can be broken down into the smaller steps that already start with your intent as you greet someone. Now ask yourself, when you say to someone "how are you," do you mean it? Do you even care about the answer? In the African bushveld, there is a tree called a Buffalo Thorn, or in Afrikaans, it is called "Blink-Blaar-Wag-n-Bietjie," which means "wait a bit." This tree is so apt as a symbolic gesture to life and relationships, because if you get caught in the thorns of this branch, which is shaped in a zig zag pattern, you have to wait a bit. (Below, you see a photo of the Blink-Blaar-Wag-n-Bietjie twig. If you want to see this and other pictures of this tree, in full colour and larger, then go to my website, www.connectedrainmaker.com, to download the full-size, full-colour, print-ready version.)

The analogy shared from so many of the local people is that this is like our lives. It is never a straight road. It is never without its twists and turns. Fascinatingly, the two thorns represent two ways of looking at our journey. The one points backwards, in remembrance of the journey that we've travelled, what we've learned and who has travelled with us—the relationships that have got us to where we

For bonuses go to ...

are—and it's a fundamental reflection at any turning point in our lives, to remember where we've come from and who we know.

The second thorn is pointing forward to say: Who do you want to take with you? Who's going on the journey from here? What's important to you and what's significant? What's sparking your battery and what's charging your energy? What's fueling your purpose? That journey is equally important. Interestingly, every turning point produces leaves. And on every leaf, there are three vines.

The first vein is the relationship with ourselves. The real me versus the ego "I"—what's the state of that relationship? Who am I really?

The second vein of that leaf represents the relationships we have with others, and that we are only human beings in the context of other human beings—that wonderful African concept of Ubuntu.

And the third key relationship is the relationship we have with something bigger, something more of meaning, something of our environment, something that drives purpose, something way beyond what we could even measure. For some, this is the relationship with their higher power, God.

A greeting is a connecting point from one human being to another, and the starting of the relationship. These connecting points are often missed due to our continuous business. It is those connection points that really bring value and significance to all the people that we are touching—not physically touching but emotionally or energetically—as we engage with them throughout the day or throughout our lives.

The Shelf Packer Named Philemon

> *"It is literally true that you can succeed best and quickest by helping others to succeed."*
> – Napoleon Hill

If you are born in a township in South Africa, or in a village in Africa, it's very difficult for you to be financially successful. If you don't have an intervention of some sort, it is often said that a big part of being successful in Africa is luck. If somebody notices you—let's say you're a good rugby player—and they then take you and put you in the right place, this would mean you have luck on your side. However, often this is not the case. Still, despite the odds, most Africans, when given a chance, will pay it forward, and this is about the essence of relationships and its meaning in the African continent.

Frans, a friend of mine, shared a beautiful life experience with me about this "pay it forward" attitude. When he worked for Hypermarket, they started an academy for young people to come and learn about franchising. They were put through a 2-year course, and this was supported with practical experience on the floor. A young man called Philemon, who was a merchandiser, a shelf packer in one of their hypermarkets, approached Frans and asked him if he could please be considered to become one of the students in this programme. Frans challenged him and asked him what he believed he could bring to this opportunity, and Philemon, without hesitation, responded and said that he was excellent, that he had been observing and learning in his job as a shelf packer, and that he knew many things, but he just needed the opportunity to prove it to someone.

Frans decided to take a chance on Philemon and put him through the programme. He was a great student and was very eager to move forward with opening a franchise in Braamfontein, Johannesburg. In order to open a business in Braamfontien, he had to invest ZAR7

For bonuses go to ...

million, to set up the shop. With Frans's guidance, he approached First National Bank, and they gave him the ZAR7 million loan to open the store. Philemon went on to run that store for 10 years, and he did very well. He almost spent 24 hours a day working in that business; he was very grateful for the opportunity. A couple of years ago, Philemon came to Frans and told him that he had decided to sell the business. For those of you that have run a supermarket before, you would know that one can only run a business like that for a certain amount of years; it's a very taxing business to run.

The good news was that he was able to sell the business for 10 times what he had paid for it. Frans smiled as he told me about this success story, and the expression on his face was clearly that of happiness and pride. He said to me that when Philemon had started this business, he had told him to please not buy a fancy car with the money, but to use it to build his business; and when Philemon sold it ten years later, he said to Frans: "Do you think I have earned the right to buy that fancy car now?" Priceless. The important part of the story is not only that a talented but hard-working man got the opportunity to excel. It gets more rewarding than that...

Philemon decided that he wanted to move back to the township where he had come from, to assist other young people to set up businesses. He wanted to pay it forward. It all goes back to the values of the African village and that we do things for others; we make a decision because it's going to be beneficial for all the people concerned, not just for one person, meaning "I," but for the whole community. The principle of the relationship mix was clear to me. He started by focusing on quality, and then with a strong foundation of trust and a clear intent to serve, Philemon was able to expand the quality contribution to quantity, through the power of Ubuntu, which I have already told you about. The spirit of Ubuntu translates into the "we culture" context; as a reminder, it says: "I am because you are."

This story reminded me of words of wisdom from the late Nelson Mandela, whom I had the privilege of meeting a few times. He said: *"What counts in life is not the mere fact that we've lived. It is what difference we made to the lives of others that will determine the significance of the life we lead."*

5 Steps to Building My Relationship Currency

"When your dreams include service to others—accomplishing something that contributes to others—it also accelerates the accomplishment of that goal. People want to be part of something that contributes and makes a difference."
– Jack Canfield

Whatever your approach is, quality or quantity, the real important question to ask yourself is, if you got out your phone right now, and you sent a text to 10 people, saying the following statement: "You are one of the most important people in my life, and I value our relationship at the highest level," would you have enough people that you would feel comfortable to text? Because the only way you're sending that text is if you truly have a relationship with that person. Otherwise, they will think something really weird is going on. But to somebody that you really have a deep connection and relationship with, you can send that text to right now, and it would be special. They will understand it, and they will respond back to you.

There are **five steps** that I take big corporate and government departments through when I help them to review their organisational strategy, and when leveraging their relational strategy. I go through these five steps when I work with high profile CEOs, presidents of countries, and entrepreneurs, and now I am using the same five steps and sharing them with you.

For bonuses go to ...

The first step is around understanding the **origin and the principles of building** your connectedness, your network of relationships; so, your leadership currency. So where does that come from? Why are relationships even important?

The second step is about having the right **mindset** to engage and build your relationship network, because without that mindset, we don't follow through successfully.

The third step will be where we build your **connector strategy**. Here, you have to be clear on what direction you want to go in, in order to build a strategy. Now, I don't want you to think that this is plastic, or that it's not real. You might be asking yourself the question: "How do I build a strategy on who I'm going to meet?" Okay, so it sounds a bit unconventional at first, maybe. So let me be clear. It doesn't mean that you don't meet people every day, like you used to before; not at all. But remember, when we put focus into a clear direction, it significantly increases our chances to achieve our large goals. And part of this focus is about putting the adequate planning in place, in order to make sure that it materialises. So when I refer to building my strategy, what I mean is, over and above the people that you will meet anyway on a daily basis, you're going to do some deliberate planning around who some of the people are that you should be meeting, that will also want to buy into your vision. And you can collectively work at making a very big impact in this world. Remember the lesson from the Zulu chief: Together or united—in other words, in teams—you are much stronger than on your own, and for the same reason, you're going to make a larger impact in teams than on your own. Alone, you might touch 1000 people in a year, but if you go and you build a strategy, and you get enough people that share in your vision, you might then impact 100,000 people. So all that we are doing, knowing that nothing is false about this process, is that we are going to do the preparation and planning around who those like-minded people are that you might need in this process, or that might want to share in your process, in order for you to scale and serve much more people on the journey. Does that make sense?

So let me maybe use this as an example. Let's say you wanted a healthy lifestyle. I don't mean a diet, and I don't mean it's about weight; I mean, living a healthy lifestyle. So yes, part of that is being within a reasonable weight. But more importantly, you focus on getting the right minerals and the right vitamins; you make sure that your acidic levels are not too high, and you're doing the required movement and exercise that you need. From a mental perspective, you may be doing some meditation or some relaxation exercises to help you clear your mind. You might use essential oils to stimulate the health centres, physically and mentally. Would you agree that in order to make sure you get all of this done, you would have to put some strategy in place? At the very least, you have to plan to buy healthy groceries to put in your cupboard. If you only had fast food, and if you only ate take-out, it wouldn't be that great; it would be very difficult for you to achieve your goal of having a healthy lifestyle if you didn't put the strategy in place to support your success. You thus look at the relationships you want to engage in to enhance the chances for success.

Then the fourth step will be to do the right research and the planning to develop and execute a **connector action plan**. Here, you will reach out to the people that you think you can bring value to, who might be interested in participating in what you would like to do.

And then the last step, step number five, is **taking action**, followed by maintenance and growth. You're going to learn exactly how to actually access the right people, but in a good way, not in a way that you are using people—in a way that you're building relationships, so that there's mutual exchange and mutual value and benefit.

For bonuses go to www.connectedrainmaker.com

Let's go on to the next chapter to get you started on executing your FIVE STEP CONNECTOR PROCESS. We will start with step number one, understanding the origin and the principles of building your connectedness, your network of relationships.

Chapter 6

Getting Started on My Connected Journey

The Origin of Connector Currency – The Reptilian Brain

> *"A deep sense of love and belonging is an irreducible need of all people. We are biologically, cognitively, physically, and spiritually wired to love, to be loved, and to belong. When those needs are not met, we don't function as we were meant to. We break. We fall apart. We numb. We ache. We hurt others. We get sick."*
> – Brené Brown

The first part of the conversation, Step 1, is about the origin and the principles of building connector currency. If we look at the history of connection, and essentially the origin, and the principles around relationship building, I want you to think back, not three, not four or not even 500 years back, but more in the region of 800 or 900 years back, before Western civilization, and when human beings were all still on the African continent. I'm sure you all know that the human race originated in Africa, and every single one of us are actually African. That is, if we go back to our ancestry, thousands of years back, at the existence of humankind.

For bonuses go to ...

In that timeframe, we were created in a way that developed something in us called the reptilian brain. Through evolution, that part of our brain still exists. That is the part of the brain that when you are in danger, it tells you to either fight or take flight, and run away. It's that same part of the brain that creates anxiety for you if you are at school and you are not fitting in. Or you feel you don't have friends, or you don't feel like you belong, or people are not nice to you and push you out; you're not part of the cool group, you don't have the right clothes or the right car, or you feel like no one has your back. People often want to belong. That sense of wanting to belong, to be part of a group, is not something shallow or unfounded. It's something that was designed in our brain at the existence of humankind, which at the time had a very important function.

Imagine you were faced with the African Big Five (lions, elephants, rhinos, leopards and buffalo), or any kind of animal that is potentially a predator to humans. Imagine further, the fact that you are also competing for the fruits and the vegetables and the food available to you, with all the other herbivores, which are often much bigger than you, or much smarter, potentially, than humans in the wild. I can tell you, if you try to climb a tree with a monkey, that monkey is going to get to the guava, or to the apple or to the orange, before you do; they are just quicker and smarter than us. I have had the opportunity to run a race with a cheetah, and believe me when I say that I had hardly left the starting point, and the cheetah had already reached the winning line. If you want to see a photo of me with a cheetah, go to www.connectedrainmaker.com to download the full-size, full-colour, print-ready version.

And so, if you think about it like that, the only way that the human race could continue to exist, or the highest chance for you to survive during those times, was to be in a tribe or in a community. Human beings are mammals, and just like other mammals, they were always in larger groups. And that was a protective mechanism. The reptilian brain would shout out, "Danger, danger, danger, and if for some reason the tribe pushed you out and said, "You are no longer part of our tribe," you knew instinctively that you were at risk to possibly die.

Take that scenario to today, many hundreds of years later in today's world. We mostly don't live in tribes anymore, and we mostly don't live in the African bush, where there's potentially immediate danger. The environment we live in today is reasonably safe from other animal predators, because we are at the top of the food chain—we designed it that way, rightly or wrongly. So today, we are not as conscious of the necessity to be in tribes or communities to be safe.

A lot of people live a more individualized approach to life in our modern society. But the one thing that has not changed is that part of your brain, the reptilian brain. So as soon as you feel like you don't have a tribe—you don't have a community of friends, or you don't have family, or you don't have people around you that have your back—it creates great anxiety. For some people, it can even create such great fear that it could even result in suicide or other terrible outcomes. I am sharing this history with you, because I want you to understand that this essence of community, of being part of a tribe, of building communities, is not a new concept. In some ways, it has just become an unconscious or forgotten concept. We moved away from it in Western society. And now we are starting to realize that those that are succeeding, those that are feeling fulfilled in their lives, are those that actually keep that element in their lives. We are starting to slowly but surely move back to that. Many people have difficulty making that transition.

The fact that you and I are having this conversation in regard to connectedness, at this particular time in your life path, gives you a huge competitive advantage. Exploring the essence of what you can achieve when you team up with other people, around one common goal to achieve something magnificent and meaningful, is a worthwhile exploration. Continue reading to hear the story of how the power of community saved a wildlife ecosystem.

For bonuses go to ...

The Himba Poacher

> *"We cannot seek achievement for ourselves
> and forget about progress and prosperity for our community...
> Our ambitions must be broad enough to include the aspirations and
> needs of others, for their sakes and for our own."*
> – Cesar Chavez

What I discovered was that human energy lies at the centre of all human outcomes. Everything we do—dancing, running, fishing, cooking, driving, sleeping, eating, writing, singing, and so on—is affected by our energy. Unfortunately, there's a flipside to positive energy, and that's negative energy. And that causes our energy to slump. By understanding some of the fundamentals on how energy works, we can support ourselves and our mindset, to propel ourselves forward into the right direction. What do I mean by this? I want you to know that energy is infectious. Yours affects mine. And mine affects yours. The fascinating thing is that ours together affects all others. We have spoken already about the simple maths of energy, so I want to remind you that we have people who add energy, and multipliers who enhance energy. And when these people get together, the energy between them just rises and rises. And the opposite happens too; when the subtractors and the dividers get together, the energy slumps. You want to keep your energy rising and rising, at least the majority of the time. Can you see why it starts being important to know what impact the people around you are having on you, and you on them? Mark Twain said: "Twenty years from now, you will be more disappointed by the things that you didn't do, than by the things that you did do. So throw off the bowlines, sail away from the safe harbour, catch the trade winds in your sails, and explore, dream and discover." Why do high energy people outperform those whose energy is low? It's because when your energy is high, your brain works better—it's as simple as that; your brain works better. And now we're going to move to the next and most important question: Where does energy come from?

Well, it comes from relationships:

- The real me and the real you, which is **trust**.
- The real me and the real us, which is about a **sense of belonging**.
- And most important, the real me and the ego selves, which is about **balance**.

After considering where it comes from, we also have to ask ourselves how we get this energy when we need it most. Well, our answers are simple. **You act in more collaborative, higher trusting ways, and in less self-serving, potentially distrusting ways.**

Instead of just telling you about the concept of "the power of infectious energy," let me tell you about a real life situation that happened not too long ago, to show the importance and the critical nature of actually having the ability to impact people in a constructive or destructive way. The story I want to share with you plays out in a country north of South Africa, in the southwestern part of Africa, called Namibia. To give you some reference, Namibia has 2.1 million people, but it is only twice the size of California. And in Namibia, a gentleman from the Himba tribe, a trained conservationist, Mr. John Kasaona, understood this concept of energy exchange between people, and the value of relationships; and he used his wisdom to channel the power of trust-based, authentic relationships into a situation that impacted more than just himself and his immediate surroundings.

You see, at a given time in Namibia, due to a complex result of actions, poaching was continuing to be on the uprise; wildlife was disappearing, which also meant less tourism future focused, and the situation seemed very hopeless. Death and despair surrounded John and his entire community. In Namibia, there are a lot of wild animals, including the Big Five. This is one of the most prominent reasons why Namibia attracts tourists, because of its ecology. It has a very unique ecology, with deserts and big sand dunes. It has an interesting

For bonuses go to ...

coastline, which is quite unique. So as wildlife is poached, it has a huge impact on the Namibian economy. Amidst this doom and gloom situation, John was able to see how to move forward with a focus on relationships. At a time when other countries with poaching challenges were shooting poachers dead, he suggested that they approach poachers from within the communities, and ask them to help with the conservation of the very animals they were hunting. Does this seem controversial? Maybe, but the irony is that this initial step of good faith helped men reclaim their ability to manage their communities' rights to own and manage wildlife. So, people that previously were poachers, became the caretakers. And thus, as people started feeling ownership over wildlife, wildlife numbers started coming back, and that has since become a foundation for conservation in Namibia.

With independence, the whole approach of community getting involved has now been embraced by the Namibian government. Three things helped to build on this foundation.

The very first one was honouring tradition and being open to new ideas. In Himba tradition, there is a sacred fire from which the spirit of their ancestors speak, through the chief, and it advises them where to get water, where to get grazing and where to go and hunt. This tradition was honoured in the new way of implementing nature conservation.

The second element was that the know-how of the poachers was now used to support the community and to protect their wildlife, and so they become respected again by the community, which allowed them to become part of their village and their people again, gaining a sense of community once more.

And lastly, partnerships were created, including with the Namibian government, with business communities in Namibia and with the World Wildlife Fund.

What started as a hopeless situation, through the building of relationships, resulted in a very small group of community rangers getting community involved, which has since grown into conservancies.

Conservancies are legally instituted by the government, and these are run by the communities themselves, for their benefit. Today, they have 60 conservancies that manage and protect over 13 million hectares, of land in Namibia. Subsequently, the entire country's' conservation has been reshaped. Nowhere else in the world has community-adopted conservation grown at this scale. This is the power of energy management and relationship building, using the only real leadership currency, the power of connectedness. This is an example to show you that the way in which you show up will very likely impact how someone else will respond back to you. Something to think about, isn't it?

Clash of the Cultures

> *"If you talk to a man in a language he understands, that goes to his head. If you talk to him in his language, that goes to his heart."*
> – Nelson Mandela

Another story I want to share with you about the importance of energy flow in a relationship, is an experience I had with a friend of mine, Coleman. Coleman is a Zulu man. We were working together on a project for one of the Fortune 500 companies. We had to go and see the managing director for the Africa region, at their head office in Johannesburg, which was in a big skyscraper building. The part of the story I want to share with you is what happened after the meeting, when Coleman and I were in the elevator (the lift, as we call it in South Africa), on our way down to the ground floor. I don't know if you've ever stood in a lift, and when you are with people that you know,

For bonuses go to ...

everyone is talking. And if someone else gets in the elevator, suddenly everyone's quiet. I'm sure you know what I am talking about... everyone then suddenly stares into nothingness.

This is exactly what happened to us. The elevator stopped at the 5th floor, and a Zulu lady entered. What made the event even funnier was that this silly little tune was playing in the elevator, a much diluted version of some classical Mozart type of music, and it was really not great. So imagine that everyone is staring into the abyss, and this music is playing in the background... Can you imagine it? Eventually, we reached ground level, and the lady stepped out of the elevator. You will understand the relevance in a moment.

As we reached the ground floor, I thought that I would be courteous, so I took a small step back so that she could see that I was letting her walk out first, because I was waiting with Coleman. So, I stepped to the side, and she walked out and went her own way. And then Coleman and I proceeded to exit and walk out of the building. When we got to the middle of the foyer, Coleman suddenly stopped and made a loud expression: "EISHHHHH Nomvula!!" Now remember, Coleman is a Zulu gentleman. I said, "What's wrong, Coleman?" He responded by saying that the situation was a very, very awkward and difficult position for him. I was confused and asked Coleman what he was talking about. We had just been in the lift. No one had said a word. We just went down the lift and we walked into the foyer.

"Difficult situation? What are you talking about?" I said. He responded and said to me, "You didn't see what was going on?" I shrugged. I had no idea what he was talking about. And he said, "But Nomvula, you are practically Zulu, and you know our culture so well. So how did you not catch that?" I still had no idea what he was talking about. I retraced our steps and said that we had merely come down the elevator, and we had then walked into the foyer, and no one had said a word. And that was all I could remember. He said, "No, no, no, you don't understand; I had to make a very strategic decision!"

Now I was really puzzled. So I said, "Coleman, I'm sorry, you're going to have to explain to me, step by step. Connect the dots for me, because I'm not following you." Coleman smiled and said, "Well, I had to make a strategic decision, because I had to decide if I was going to upset the other lady or you, because I couldn't make both of you happy." Now I was even more confused. I said, "Coleman, you need to explain more. You didn't even say anything to me or to her." What I did not take into consideration was that this lady was also a Zulu lady, so that was the relevance. Something that you might not know about the Zulu culture is that a Zulu man takes pride in the fact that, as a gentleman, he would walk out first, culturally, and let the woman follow him. This is where the trick comes in.

Coleman became very passionate and demonstrative, and said to me, "You know, Nomvula, the Western man says to the woman, you go first. And if I see everything is okay, nothing has killed you out there, I'll follow you." He said, "I find that ridiculous; and in Western culture, you call that gentlemanly behaviour. You expect the woman to take the first step into the danger zone, and then you follow her."

He started laughing. He smiled and said proudly, "I am proud to remain in my Zulu tradition. I say to the woman, 'You stand back, woman; let me check what is out there first. If everything is safe, you can follow.'" And so, this was the dramatic, playful way in which he explained the dynamics of a gentleman to me. Coleman wanted to be a gentleman to us both, but he could not respect Zulu culture and respect Western culture simultaneously, because it required the opposite behaviour, and he couldn't do them both at the same time—hence, it was a tough spot to be in.

Finally, he said to me, "Well, I decided that I was spending the rest of the day with you, so I made sure that you were happy." Today, I am very aware of this cultural dilemma. If I'm with a Zulu man, I will take a step back when they walk towards the door, so that they can see that I understand, for them to be a gentleman to me, they will walk

For bonuses go to ...

out first, and I will follow. And so that's my way of supporting authentic relationships, by taking the time to understand others.

So very often, by informing yourself and becoming more aware of other people's cultures and their approach to doing things, it can really be a relationship builder. Think of how you have felt in the past if someone took the time to understand where you were coming from. When I speak about community and relationships, accountability of self is very important. And that's the starting point before we can engage in our relationships. And if we are truly accountable for our own behaviour, we could also argue that at least partially, you choose which aspects of an individual influence you.

When you challenge your thinking, and why you think a certain way, you can be surprised by yourself. It's an incredible thing to surprise yourself. When you're in a group with people, where you are allowing yourself to really listen and reflect, you can come up with a concept, a thought, and go like, "Wow, did I come up with that? You see, at that moment, it is not about you, nor is it about them; it is about the collective experience, where you thought and you reflected while people were speaking to you. You listened to them and assimilated the discussions, and so again, the collective always brings out more brilliance than individualistic components. We now realize that energy plays a big role in relationships, but how about our mindset, the way we think about things?

Creating My Connector Mindset – My Inner Process

"In order to get what you want, you must first decide what you want. Most people really foul up at this crucial first step because they simply can't see how it's possible to get what they want, so they don't even let themselves want it."
– Jack Canfield

I would like to highlight some guidelines that you can consider as you develop your connector mindset; this is Step 2 in our connector process. We will look at it from two perspectives:

- What do I lead with from the inside?
- What do I follow with on the outside?

I want to draw from Martin Luther King Jr., who summarized beautifully what I am trying to say, when he said: "Until you have found something you're willing to die for, you're not fit to live." This is, of course, a huge commitment. But that's what vision is about. Your first tip in creating your connector mindset is about the inner empire realizing, before the outer empire. Your inner empire is about you; you're in it yourself. You can see, as I am preparing you for your connected mindset, that I've been working a lot more on the inside of you, than looking at the actual tangible strategy that we're going to be working on. But I need to prepare you, your mindset, before you start doing your strategy and action plan. Otherwise, when you start actively activating that plan, you won't get the response that you desire from the people you will be engaging.

One of the things I would like you to realize is that you'll never make more money than the value or the quality that you first have, in terms of your own identity and the value and the quality that you bring into other people's lives. So, you can't impact the world externally if you haven't worked on your inner life first. You can only give that which you have to give. That is why you start with yourself first. If you don't

For bonuses go to ...

get your inner empire right—your mind, your physical life, your physical fitness, your emotional life, your spiritual life—you cannot help with or lift everything that you touch in your outer life. You are bringing what you have inside of you, to the outside. You need to work on your inside first. So, instead of focusing on getting the right person, first become the right person.

The final tip in preparing your connector mindset from the inside, is to look at your days as if they are your life in miniature. Don't feel so overwhelmed or waste away days, because how you live today is a miniature version of how you are going to experience your life. You don't just get lucky; you make luck by planning well, and by understanding what that sharp focus is for you that you are moving towards. You need to have a laser focus and know what direction you're moving in, and then if your vision is clear, you will bring people on board. If you have vague goals, well, you will get vague results.

A lot of my coaching clients say to me that their number one goal is that they want to be happy. So, often, my response to them is, "Okay, what will make you happy?" They might mention one or two things. Then I will say to them, "Okay, if I gave it to you right now, then does that mean you will be happy for the rest of your life?" All of them say no. You see, sadly, most people don't really know fully what it means for them to be happy. Some people have said to me during coaching that they know what their number one goal is, and often they say their goal is that they want to make more money. My response is that I will give them $1. And I say, "Okay, you've made more money. Are you satisfied?" And the answer, of course, is NO!! That's not what they meant, of course, but they were vague in their goal. So I say to them, "If you are vague, then your results will be vague." So it's really important to be very clear. Clarity breeds mastery!! Success, productivity and real results are handcrafted by you and your vision. So it all starts with you!! You can learn more about how we can work together to help you and/or your business get to where you want to be, at www.connectedrainmaker.com.

Creating My Connector Mindset – My Outer Process

"Success is a science;
if you have the conditions, you get the result."
– Oscar Wilde

When focusing on the outside, to demonstrate our connector mindset, it starts with the creation of quality constructed daily habits. The first thing to consider on the outside is how you manage yourself, and then how you manage your relationships. This is done by doing small, daily acts of greatness. Doing what I'm proposing to do is not one grand gesture. Success here is more about having grit, being willing to do, day by day, the small things that are easy to do, and easy not to do. So at first, as you start changing this behaviour, it's really, really hard. And if you continue, it develops into a middle period that really feels messy at times, thinking that you don't know exactly if you're getting it or not, and asking yourself if it is really working or not. But if you persist, despite those thoughts and feelings, the transformation will happen, and once it does, everything just clicks through, and then you start receiving the benefits of this process. These personal benefits also spill over into benefiting others, your relationships and your network of connections.

Being consistent over a period of time, is another key fundamental aspect in fostering a connector mindset (some people refer to this as fractals; I have a summary for you about fractals, in the resource section on my website, at www.connectedrainmaker.com. Go have a look.). It's similar to exercise. It doesn't help if you run a marathon once a year, and then you do no other exercise for the rest of the year; that's not going to make you a healthy or fit person. You can rather do 15 minutes of exercise daily, and repeat it at least five times a week. And you're going to be healthier than someone that does one exceptional exercise routine but then does nothing for the rest of the year. It's the same with building relationships. It's small, steady improvements in the race. What I like to call this is your genius capability of building relationships. And genius is not about genetics. It's about the habits that you create. It's about the devotion. You have your relentlessness and your commitment to follow through on that vision that you've put in place. Success is a lot more about relentlessness and grit, and less about natural talent.

The next tip says that icons aren't busy. You know, this is something that I've found interesting. There's this dynamic in the world where it's very modern and very trendy, and very cool to say, "Oh, I'm so busy." Really, what you are saying is that you don't know how to manage your time. That's really what you are saying. What I want to highlight to you is that to be "busy being busy," is really saying that you haven't fully grasped what it is to lead your own life. And if you don't know how to lead your own life, it will be very difficult to lead people at the level of the impact that I think you would like to make. If you look at some of the greatest icons, they are some of the biggest figures in terms of contribution. In fact, they have a lot of free time, and that free time is not sitting watching Netflix or doing nothing. But that free time is time that they've scheduled to sit and think, to reflect, to identify and find and research some solutions. They're not just running from one activity to the other.

If you want to achieve something of real magnificence, don't make a list of 50 or 100 different goals or tasks that you want to achieve. If that is what you want to do, you need to create the teams first, which is part of what I'm teaching you to do. But until you've got those teams in place, the most successful people only have four or five major goals. And that may be one obsessive mission. So that one major thing is what drives you every day of your life. What you do is that you remove the complexity of all the demand on your time and your work, and you create more simplicity. This is how you win at making the impact that you really want to make.

Finally, you can have everything, have everything you like, but don't be in the position where you need anything. And I mean from a physical or material perspective. So very often today, the popular thing is the glitz and glamour. Everyone wants the bling. Everyone wants all the beautiful stuff. You can have it but still live your life in a way that you are in the world, but not of the world. What I'm trying to say is, enjoy the pleasures. Of course, that's what they are there for. But don't be attached to them; don't run after those things with everything you have, and lose focus or forget about what else is important.

The Big Five, the Little Five and the Micro Five

> *"Give me six hours to chop down a tree and I will spend the first four sharpening the axe."*
> – Abraham Lincoln

If clarity does breed mastery, then how do we get this clarity thing going? We know our mindset needs to be right, and we spoke about the connector mindset. We also know that we need to have focus.

As you know, we have the Big Five in South Africa. In the context of preparing and finding our focus, I like to think of my major goals, my focus on my life journey, as my **Big Five**. **I ask myself what the five things are that need to happen between today and the end of my life, that will make me feel like I have lived a legendary life.** Please make a note of this, and start thinking about what your answer is to that question. What are your Big Five?

Dr. Demartini highlights that our life goal is highly impacted and informed by our hierarchy of values. So, the next thing that I need to be clear on is what my **five key values of my life are, that inform everything that I do**. What are those values that you will not change? They are fundamental in your life, and I call them my **Little Five**. You might think that I made up the term "Little Five," but no, I didn't!! In

For bonuses go to ...

Africa, we really have something called the Little Five, and just for fun, here they are: the elephant shrew, the ant lion, the rhinoceros beetle, the buffalo weaver and the leopard tortoise.

Then the last one in the series of fives, is what I call the **Micro Five**. These are **your daily five actions you are focusing on towards achieving your Big Five**. Every morning, write down five little wins that you'll achieve. It can be something different: "I'll smile at someone that looks like they're having an unhappy day," or, "I will call a client and wish them a happy birthday." Just five little things. If you are wondering when you should start with all of this, the right answer is 20 years ago, but you can't do that. So, the second best answer is to start today; just take imperfect action.

You might feel tired right now, but I still want to encourage you to please do the steps. Don't wait for another day; you will always be busy, and it will never be at the right time, but you need to create time for yourself—you are worth it.

As part of this introspective journey, the last part that I want you to look at is, "Why are you here on Earth?" To reflect on this very large question, I have put together a list of sub-questions for you to reflect on, to gain more clarity:

- What do you think is your purpose?
- What contribution were you born to make?
- What do you think is something that you can contribute that no one else can do as well as you?
- What burning desire lies deep within your soul?
- What are some goals that you really want to achieve in this life?
- What are you doing right now that is putting a smile on your face? I want you to think about that, because if it isn't, why isn't it? And if it isn't, what would? What do you need to change about it?
- Are you excited about the present and the future?

- What is your biggest challenge right now? What is that one thing that you're really struggling with? It might not be one; it might be a few things. That's why I say "biggest" challenges.
- Do you have a vision?
- Do you have a mission?
- Do you have your values in mind? If you do, please write them down.
- What did you do today that took you one step closer to your infinite magnificence? What is that step? And remember, I said to use small, daily actions. It's not about something that's grand and large—just a small action.
- Do you have clear direction?
- Are you committed?

Elon Musk, a South African, whom I think most of you know, says the following: *"I think it's possible for ordinary people to choose to be extraordinary."* I want to make that invitation to you. I believe that you might feel ordinary today, but you can choose to become extraordinary. And the way in which you do that is by really understanding yourself better. Once your mindset is right, you are ready to start working on your connector strategy. Let's explore this together in the next chapter.

Chapter 7

My Connector Strategy

River Rafting in Colorado

> *I believe that people make their own luck by great preparation and good strategy."*
> – Jack Canfield

You need to have clarity around what direction in life and in business you want to move into. This clarity will inform how you move through the process of building a connector strategy and a connector action plan. Every plan will be different, depending on where you want to go and what direction you want to take.

It's a great time to be alive. We have so many opportunities and choices, so many options. The real challenge is to know how to choose what you really want to do. How do you choose what it is that you really want to contribute? Because there are just so many things you can and maybe want to do, right? You might feel that you are in that position of asking yourself which one you should do, and which one you should wait to do. There are just so many things you can consider, can choose or can become. If you have too many choices, and you lack focus—and believe me, I've learned the hard way—then you won't get traction; you need to focus and be sure. Have one or a maximum of two things that you focus on until they start getting momentum. Only then can you bring in new things. I've got this tool called the

For bonuses go to ...

"clarity mapping tool," which I want to share with you; it's a tool that helps you to set a very clear intention, and to get laser clear and laser sharp on the direction you want to go in life. Essentially, the Clarity Mapping Tool helps you to address the direction that you want to take. Now why is this even important?

Dean Graziosi shared an experience with me that informed the creation of the Clarity Mapping Tool. The story started with a gentleman called Ethan Willis. Ethan Willis is a church leader. In America, some of the church groups take the children away on summer camps during summer break, which is usually over June and July. One of these tutors, over this specific summer break, was Ethan Willis. As I said, he was the church leader. He had a group of dads, the fathers that were taking their children to the camp. Approximately 20 children were going together in a group, to a summer camp. All of these children were between the ages of 15 and 17 years old. What they were going to do was to go white river rafting in the Colorado River. It was a church adventure trip.

Just before they left for this trip, it rained a lot in Colorado; so much so, that the waters were really quite aggressive, to the point where the fathers of these children were looking at the water and saying that they didn't know if they should go ahead with the adventure. If they had to rate the rapids, it would be a five out of five, and they were about to cancel the entire white river rafting. Then the guide came out, and he said to the dads: "Wait, wait, wait; relax. I want to tell you to please don't cancel this. I want the boys to climb into the raft, and I'll tell you why." He said, "All I want them to do is to do exactly what I say, and everything will be fine. I will point my finger in a direction. And if I point my finger in that direction, all I want the boys to do is take all their energy and focus. They must row and row, and paddle and paddle with all their energy and attention. At that moment, they must give it all they have, all their energy and all their focus as a team. And he said, "I promise you that you will be safe if you just go in the direction that I point to." And then he said jokingly, "Well, at least I've never lost anyone yet." Then he went on to explain, "Well, you know what I did in the beginning? I used to have a group of boys, and I would say to them to climb onto the raft, and we would start going down the river. If I saw a big tree in the water, I would tell them to be careful, and I would point to the tree. Or if we passed a rock, I would tell them to be careful of the rock." And he said, "Lo and behold, every time I showed them the tree, and every time I showed them the rock, they would smash right into it."

What he started realizing was that at the moment that he pointed it out to them, everyone would look at that thing, the rock or the tree or something of danger. And when they looked at it, it meant that the focus was there. If their focus was there, they went right into it. So, he thought, how do I use that to my advantage? If I know that what they focus on is where they go, all I need to do is point them in the direction in which I know that they need to be going. This guide knew that river like the back of his hand; he knew exactly when you would have to go very wide on an angle, "because there's a water stream on this side, the current will take you like this, and then it will get you past." And so, instead, what he did was that he would point in the direction in which they should paddle, instead of pointing to what they should avoid.

Think about how this relates to you. When you think about what you want in life, or what you want in your career, or for those of you that want to be entrepreneurs, what you want in your business, wouldn't you agree with me that very often you focus on the things that you don't want? This is not just in business but also in life, in health and in our relationships; we can fill in the blanks in all kinds of parts of our lives. Very often, what we do is to be very clear on knowing for certain that we don't want this, or we don't want that. And what are we doing? We are focusing on what we don't want. And what we focus on, we get more of. The more you focus on that which you don't want, the more of it you're going to get. It's very simple to change that. You need to start focusing on what you actually do want, in the same way

For bonuses go to ...

that this guide would say, "I will point my finger where you need to go, and you just go there with all your energy, all your focus, all your effort; you just row and row, and you will miss the rocks, and you will miss the trees—you'll miss everything that you shouldn't be crashing into, because your direction is focused on where you want to go.

My Clarity Mapping Tool

*"That inner voice has both gentleness and clarity.
So to get to authenticity, you really keep going down to the bone,
to the honesty, and the inevitability of something."*
– Meredith Monk

We will go into deeper detail to build your connector strategy and gain deeper understanding of exactly what it is that you want to do with your life. Understand that it's not a decision that can never change; but for now, this will be your focus. Think about what that contribution is that you want to make at this moment in your life. I am going to share the fundamentals of the Clarity Mapping Tool with you so that you can figure this out for yourself.

The exercise that I'm going to ask you to do is about your bigger picture. It's about thinking about what the direction is that you really want to take. In the chapters ahead, we will then build on this as we move through the 5 steps. This way, you know that you're actually going to achieve that which you want to do. You can avoid all the things that aren't going to build the life, or the bigger future, or the career, or the business that you actually want. You can focus on those things that you actually want. I encourage you to be honest with yourself. No one is going to ask you for the answers to your questions in this process, but I do want you to please take it seriously. Don't say that you'll do it later; please do it now. Here are some of the questions I am going to ask you to think about as you use your Clarity Mapping Tool.

Please, can you go ahead and think about the following questions:

The first question is: **What is your current truth?** Meaning, what is your current status? So, what do you feel is your lifeline right now? Just for a moment, you have the opportunity to say, "Okay, this is my reality." And maybe, in your reality, there are some things that you don't want. If we look at the story I just shared with you about Ethan Willis, part of their current truth was that there had been a lot more rain than what they had expected, which for them meant very aggressive rapids. So those are things that you don't ideally want. What are your current truths? What is your current status?

The second thing I want you to look at is **your one-year goal**. I want you to write a letter to yourself. Think of it as if your future self is writing you a letter, looking back over the last year, and telling you everything that you've achieved. You think of yourself as if you are now in your time zone a year from now. Let's say it is actually now April 2021; then, you think of yourself as being in April 2022, looking back one year. You are sharing everything that you've achieved in this one year, up to April 2022, with your current self (the self from April 2021).

The third step is: **Why are these goals important?** Why did you want to achieve them in this year ahead? Why do you think that they are important? That's your motivation. That's what's going to make you wake up in the morning, like me being here with you through your process, almost like a virtual coach through these pages, and I am here because I care about how you lead as a present and future generation leader. I care about how you are going to stand up as leader. And I believe that if you are reading this book and going through the process, you have selected yourself to stand up and make a difference. This means you are one of the chosen ones. I want to help you with the experience that I have, because I want you to fast-track your impact in this world. I'm here because I really want to help you

For bonuses go to ...

succeed, by sharing my experiences and the shortcuts I wish someone had shared with me.

And then the last question I want you to think about is: **What capabilities do you need in order to achieve that goal?** Remember, you're looking at your goal one year from now, what you would have achieved, and you are also thinking about why it's important, and you are thinking about the skills or capabilities that you don't have in your current state right now, which you will have to build or that you'll have to learn in order to achieve the goal one year from now. I want you to give more thought about what direction you actually want to move into, and to have a very laser-sharp focus, so that when you get to the point where you build the strategy, you are clear as to where you want to go. This Clarity Mapping Tool helps you to gain very clear, laser-sharp focus on how to move forward. I have prepared a Clarity Tool Worksheet for you, which you can download from my website at www.connectedrainmaker.com, to complete this process.

As a note of inspiration to take on the challenge and complete your clarity tool, listen to these wise words by Oscar Wilde: "*To live is the rarest thing in the world; most people just exist, that's all.*" What I wish for you is that you feel like you live, not that you just exist.

Connector Strategy – The Big Who

> "*When someone shows you who they are, believe them the first time.*"
> – Maya Angelou

The first step in building your connector strategy is about gaining clarity on who you want to impact. I want you to take a moment to reflect on the people that have helped you in your life, the people that have helped you on your path; all of us have them. Think about great moments in your life, where it was because one person helped you, or one person believed in you, or one person gave you a little piece of advice, or opened a door for you, and it changed your life. Who is that someone for you?

These moments can have a huge impact, or it could be small. A close friend of mine recently shared an experience when I asked him this question, and although I know him very well, I didn't know this about him. When he was a young child, he absolutely loved dancing, and he dreamt of being a dancer at a very young age. Today, he's already in his early 50s. In many cultures, a few decades ago, it would be frowned upon if a little boy wanted to do. He didn't want to only do ballroom dancing; he wanted to do ballet, modern dancing, hip hop and every style of dance you can think of. He just loved dancing. He also was from a loving family, but his parents couldn't really afford the dancing classes that he so much wished he could do. He realized, although his mother was supportive of him wanting to do dancing, this would soon become the end, because he knew that she couldn't afford it. He didn't want to put that burden on her, or ask her, because he just knew that she couldn't; she couldn't make ends meet.

He went on to tell me—and his face brightened up when he shared this with me—"You know, Ezanne, my dancing teacher saw something in me; she saw the talent that I had, and she created the opportunity for me." Through his whole childhood, without him ever asking, or without the parents ever asking (she must have realized that his parents were not able to pay), he participated in the dancing classes until he was a young adult, for free. She helped him and she supported him, and she taught him how to dance. And when he was a young adult, he then applied internationally and became an international dancer. This one kind moment or act, from one human being to another—the "power of who"; and in his case, his dancing teacher—formed and shaped his entire career. If she had not offered that free service, that value contribution to him, by offering him the opportunity to be a dancer, his life would never have unfolded as it has today. For him, that was his significant story. What is your significant story?

Understanding the "power of who" is critical for real success-driven relationships. When we get stuck, we often say, what must I do? Or, how must I do this? I want to urge you to stop asking the "what" and the "how" first. The first question you should ask is "who"—*who* is the person that knows how to do this? It's very important to start building this habit as early on as possible in your life, because what we tend to do is that we tend to say that it's going to cost too much money. So you would rather not ask people, because you don't have the money to pay them. You try and do everything yourself. You are hampering yourself.

Now, in order to feel confident to identify the "who" and then act upon it, the next step is equally important: You need to think about how you can bring value to other people. To pay someone is one way to bring value to someone, but there are many alternatives that you can consider as ways to bring value to people. What you want to do is to build this habit of over-delivering—bringing people a lot of value, leading with generosity—when you start a relationship. What I mean by that is, think about how you can help the other person when you are engaging a new relationship; don't lead with what you think they can do for you. Do you understand? I have prepared a "Connector Strategy – The Big Who" worksheet for you, which you can download at www.connectedrainmaker.com, to complete this process.

You don't have to be born into relationships; you can actually create the relationships that you really desire, but first you have to figure out how you can serve or bring value to that person, based on their needs. When I was very young, I didn't fully understand this. My father, who I've mentioned to you before, was someone that was loved by 1000s and 1000s of people. And he lived most of his life in a time that didn't really have internet and social media. But I can tell you that at his funeral, there were people from four different continents, who flew specially to be at the funeral to show their respects to him. And this shows the power of how he conducted his life. He taught me a lot about the value of being authentic, and the value of building relationships. When I was little, I didn't fully understand that.

Often, he would want to contact someone to help me open a door to do something I was aspiring towards. I would always say to him, "No, daddy, you must not call them, because I don't want the advantage above other people whose parents might not know everyone." I missed the point, right? I still had to do the work, I still had to show up, I still had to be professional, I still had to be someone worthwhile for them to want to help me—all my father would have done was open the door for me. It was only in my later adult years that I realized that it's okay to accept the help from the people that you built the relationships with, because that is really where your currency lies.

I call this the real leadership currency; the stronger the relationships, the higher the ability to influence. You can have people that are not necessarily wealthy, but they have high influence because they are connected to so many people. So don't fool yourself. Don't think that it's only the wealthy people that open up doors. It can be every single human being, but it is based on the quality of your relationship with another human being. So, the first step in building your relationship strategy, is understanding this first element of the "big who." When I speak of the "big who," I am not saying that you must look at everything that is just about you and what you need, or that you just look at who you need in order to progress in your life. No, that's not going to work. You have to lead with being genuine, being a real caring person to other human beings. You need to be caring, and you need to lead with a spirit of service, and focus on how you can help others; so, it's about being generous to other people.

Some people will keep score and say, "Well, I did these two favours for you, and you've done nothing for me yet." Don't do that. Just lead with generosity; give to people freely, and don't keep score. You might give value to person A, and then you might be surprised that they might not be able to give the value back to you. But they might know person C who knows person D, and person D is a person that will give back to you when you really need it. This is how it works. We're a connected society. When you are engaging someone because you're trying to see what you can get from them, people feel it. And it's very hard to build relationships like that. Think about it for yourself. If I met you because I wanted something from you, aren't you going to be a bit more guarded? I'm meeting you with an openness, leading with an attitude of serving you, like I am doing now—I want to help you by sharing with you the experiences I have had and the lessons I have learnt, so that your life ahead will be more prosperous, and so that your life will move faster in the direction of living a fulfilled life. It's easier to open up to such a relationship when someone is giving with an open heart, no strings attached.

Connector Strategy – The Big What

> *"I don't know what your destiny will be, but one thing I know: the only ones among you who will be really happy are those who will have sought and found how to serve."*
> – Albert Schweitzer

If being connected is the real leadership currency that we are aiming to build, then we need to understand what value we will bring to the relationship that we are building, especially since we want to lead with giving, right? Thus, the next step in our connector strategy is that we need to develop currency that matters to others. An example of building currency in my own life is that I've made many mistakes in my life, but I can tell you that I've never made the mistakes in a way that I deliberately wanted to do harm to another human being. And that is something that I'm proud of, and the people that do business with me know that about me, so I have built a high level of trust and credibility with many people. This needs to be protected of course, and valued, and this is certainly one of my currencies that I bring to a business table—trust and credibility—and this is not as common as one would hope it to be. It is about defining your value of what you will bring and how you will bring generosity to people. I'm going to ask you to start thinking of someone that you might know, but you don't know them that well, and you want to take one step closer to them, or maybe you just haven't spoken to them in a while, and you want to make the effort of connecting. Then I want you to find an opportunity to share something with this individual.

Something that I do to build caring and closeness with people is that I use my phone as a way to create closeness, by being authentic and sharing with people when I think about them. Or I might have something that I want to share with them, which I might have seen online, and which I believe would be helpful or interesting to them. Every day, I will choose at least five people, and that's my little activity that is part of my connector building process. Remember, we spoke previously about the small actions of greatness. This is one of my small actions. Maybe I'll see on social media that someone just had a baby, or it's their birthday, or they had some achievement, or something tragic happened in their life; and I will take the time, and I will care enough to send them a personal message. Does that make sense?

You can open up and be authentically you; this also brings us closer to people by sharing of ourselves. Generosity is about being of service to someone; so, really giving with an open heart. So how I see my generosity in giving to you right now as you read this book, is that I'm not sharing just a standard theoretical idea, or giving you only parts of the solution; I am giving you the tricks, the tools, the advice and the experience of things that I am using right now, at this moment. And I can tell you that a lot of what I share with you, I have personally paid for, and continue to pay 1000s of dollars to be coached. I am then choosing to coach you and share this valuable secret sauce with you. So, I know that I'm leading with generosity, because what I share with

For bonuses go to ...

you, I've had to pay in some instances to get access to, and other elements are based on my experience, which is basically my life, which I'm offering to you as part of the learning process. That's a part of leading with generosity.

But to make it a little bit easier, depending on where you are in your life, you might be thinking, "Oh, I don't know if I really have something to offer." But let's say you wanted to meet someone who's important to you, and they are in a high position in a company or in politics, or they are a celebrity—someone that's important to you. You might say, "Well, what would they want from me? What is it that I can really give to them?" Understand that there's always something that people need that you will be able to give, because you have gifts inside of you; you just don't think of it like that right now.

Let's look at it in different categories to make it easier for you. The first way I would like you to look at the value or currency that you can bring to a relationship, is in 3 layers: general, personal life or business. If we look at general currency, this is something that you can give to people freely and easily, even if you never see them again, like helping them with directions, giving them a sincere compliment, and things like that. You might walk into a shop, and you see someone you met before, and you notice that the lady has gone to the hairdresser and changed her hairstyle, and you think it looks beautiful. You can just say to her, "Well, Julie, I really love how you've changed your hairstyle; it really looks beautiful." It's that simple. That's a part of the general currency that we can draw on.

Personal currency is about leading with what matters to the other person; it's not about you. You can divide the focus into different categories of a person's life. I run a programme that uses a transformational lifestyle design system that empowers you to envision, plan and achieve your very best life, on your own terms and nobody else's. Imagine owning a 100-page book with a crystal clear vision for the person you want to become, and the life you want to live (beyond the cookie cutter goals imposed on you by society; the culturescape we spoke about). Every dream, every desire, every goal—everything that you really want—captured on the pages of your personal blueprint for life. If you want to learn more about this programme, have a look at www.connectedrainmaker.com, to participate.

An example of personal currency that I would like to share with you is something I did for my sister. She lives very far away from me, and not too long ago, she was having a complicated pregnancy; she was not allowed to move around much, she was in pain and every part of her body was swollen. She was very uncomfortable, which also affected her emotions. I wanted to make her feel pampered and loved, because she is very loved by me. I thought about her health category, and what would make her feel better, and it gave me an idea on how I could serve her and care for her. I got this idea to arrange with a very good beautician, who I know in my sister's town, to go to my sister's home to give her a foot massage and to do a facial for her. I knew that was something that she would appreciate at that time, because she didn't feel that well. It worked, and today she has a healthy baby boy.

The last category is your business currency, where you can offer your professional expertise, or a business connection; essentially, it's about offering extraordinary value to the client, by either offering a quality service or a quality product. So that's what I'm doing for you right now. Right? I'm helping you to grow in your professional life, through your relationships. That is the value I bring to you. It might be something as simple as one of your colleagues wanting to purchase a car, and you know someone that imports cars or that can get cars at a very good deal. And you just connect the two people—that is financial value. In terms of prioritisation, here is a rule of thumb you can follow in a linear time zone, on when to use which currency. We have 24 hours, so therefore, with your personal currency, you can be a bit more selective, and with your business currency, you can be more liberal than with your personal currency, but more conservative than with

For bonuses go to ...

your general currency. With general currency you should have no conservatism. You just spread the love everywhere; you just give the universal currency to anyone and everyone, even if you don't see them ever again.

I'm explaining this to you, not to impress you but to impress upon you that everything that I'm teaching you is what I use myself. I cannot emphasise enough that you really have to do it from your heart, with authenticity. If it's false, people will figure it out very quickly. You might get away with it once or twice, but once you are caught out, it's very hard to get back that confidence that people had in you. I have prepared a "Connector Strategy – The Big What" worksheet for you, which you can download at www.connectedrainmaker.com, to complete this process.

Connector Strategy – The Big Why

"A single sunbeam is enough to drive away many shadows."
– Francis of Assisi

Identify your "why." What is it that motivates you? This is really to anchor you in your soul. What is it that you want to do, and why do you want to do it? What is it that is really motivating you to do it? Why do you want to gain these capabilities? Why do you want more success? Why do you want to achieve more?

Why? Why? Why? Most people don't really know. When I coach people, they can always tell me what they don't want, but not what they do want. The problem with that is that if you keep on focusing on what you don't want, you get more of that. The "why" is, of course, identified through your understanding of identifying what the problem is that you want to solve. This one should be a little bit easier for you to think about, with the reflection you have already done, because we've already started speaking about it earlier on. If we look at someone like Elon Musk again, the reason why he is solving such great problems, is because he did this activity multiple times, identifying what the big things are in the world that no one's addressing, which he is willing to address and solve.

I want to introduce you to an exercise that is called the Seven Levels Deep Exercise. What it does is that it actually helps you to go deeper and deeper, at different levels, to get to the real "why" that motivates you, the reason you want to contribute to a particular cause, or solve a particular problem. You think you know why you want a particular thing. Ask yourself that question seven times, and be honest with yourself. Very often, I encourage people to get a partner, another human being, to ask them the "why" question, even if they don't understand the exercise. When you ask it to yourself, it's a bit difficult to get to the next level, because you have to respond from the heart, not from the mind.

Essentially, it helps you to think differently than when you are hearing your own voice asking the "why," and your own voice having to come up with a quick answer to the question. In this scenario, you constantly need to move from heart to head if you ask yourself the questions. If someone else does it, you can stay in your heart and just focus on answering honestly. So what you are trying to do, just to reiterate, is that you are trying to go from your surface level "why," to a much deeper level. So I'm going to share an example with you to illustrate what I mean. This is an example of someone that went through this seven levels deep exercise, and this is what they actually came up with.

This person asked to be coached because he really wanted to scale his business. He was already a very successful man at the time; in fact, he's a multimillionaire, but he wanted to impact more people. So in order to impact more people, it meant that he wanted to scale his business to the next level. He did not only want to be American based, but to be globally based. He wanted to understand what this would mean for him. He did the seven levels deep exercise because he really needed to understand why he is doing what he is doing, not only at the surface but at the much deeper level of what is motivating him.

It's very hard for us to get to our own answers; we need an experienced strategic advisor or an experienced coach to help us to get to those real answers. He did the exercise, and I will share with you how the conversation went. These were his actual responses. He's a well-known person; he looks very successful from the outside, and he is successful. But as I said, at that stage, he wanted to scale up, and he needed a deeper understanding of his motivation. For the purpose of the exercise, I will call him John.

Seven Levels Deep

"A champion needs a motivation above and beyond winning."
– Pat Riley

Remember, John was clear as to why he wanted to get coaching support, and he understood that his reason, his "why," was that he wanted to scale the business. This was the departure point. The next level of "why" was to ask him, "Why do you want to scale your business?" And he was like, "I don't know; I haven't really thought about this. But maybe it is that I want to make a deeper impact. I want to help more people." The next level of question was, "Why is it so important for you to help more people?" And he thought a little bit again, and he said, "Well, it's because I want to set a new standard in the industry. You know, we've all plateaued, and we believe that this is kind of where you've made it, but I want to set a new standard in my industry." Great reflection, and so the next level "why" was, "So why is it so important for you to set this new standard in your industry?" And what usually happens between level three and level four, is that people start moving from their head to their heart, okay?

The first two or three responses are intellectual responses. This is what we think it's about. But it's only when we shift things into our heart space—where we start feeling the emotions—that we start to find our real "why." When you have your real "why," nothing will stop you; you will make it happen.

So, next was to say, "So please explain to me, why do you want to set a new standard in your industry?" The shift from head to heart was evident in his eyes, and he sat back a little bit. He thought for a moment, and he sighed and said, "Well, if I'm really honest, what I'm feeling (he even used the word "feeling," so it gave a clear indication that he had shifted) is that I really want to leave a legacy." So now he was already at level five. The next level was to say, "Why is it that you want to leave a legacy?" And of course, it becomes a bit more difficult at every level for him to answer that question. And I want to tell you, the temptation is going to come where you're going to think, "No, I'm deep enough. Level five is good. I don't need to go to seven." Please remember, it's only that voice chattering in your head; you cannot stop. You have to go all the way to level seven. Okay? You are not there yet. You have to go to level seven. Next was, "Okay, so you want to scale your business because you want to leave a legacy?" Do you? Yeah, that sounds feasible. But it wasn't yet his deep, deep, deep emotional "why." So he would have stopped if the running got too hard, if that was the "why" that he was left with, but he carried on, and so the process continued, "So why is it so important for you to leave a legacy at this moment?"

At this level, something very significant happened. Tears started welling up in his eyes. He looked down, and then he looked up again. And he said, "People don't know this about me, but I come from very humble beginnings. I had a mother and father that divorced very early on in my life. And my mother did her best to take care of me. My father was not doing that well on his own. And when I was about 10 years old, I asked to go and live with my dad, because I was very worried

For bonuses go to ...

about him. My dad was not doing that well. And it went so badly that sometimes he and I would sleep together in a bath in a public bathroom, just so that we had a warm place to sleep."

And the tears started running. He said, "There were days that we didn't have food to eat. And my father was too proud, so he never asked anyone for help. And I was hungry. At the age of 10, I often went to sleep hungry, not knowing where I would sleep tomorrow; since the night before, we only had an opportunity because someone forgot to close the bathroom. We had a place to sleep."

He said, "You have no idea what that feels like. You are asking me why I want to leave a legacy. The real reason is because I never ever want to go backwards. Everyone looks at me, and they see the success. And yes, I have made financial success on a multi-millionaire level. But I know that I could make one big mistake, and it could take me back there. And I never ever want to go back."

And one could feel he was now really starting to get in touch with his feelings. The next level was (this was now level 6), "Why is it that you never want to go back there? Why don't you want to go backwards?" Again, the tears welled up, and he said, "I have kids." He said, "Do you have kids? You will know what I mean, if you have kids. I want my children to have choices. If I go backwards, what choices will they have? Not much. And I never ever want them to experience what I experienced." Now, you see, the process could have stopped at that point, but it was only level 6, so there was still one level to go.

The last level was, "So why do you want your children to have choices?" And that was when the breakthrough came. He looked up and said, "I know now what my "why" is. I want to do all of this—scale my business, make a bigger impact; I want to set a new standard in the industry, and I want to leave a legacy. Yes, because I don't want to go backwards. And yes, because I want my kids to have choices. But really, it is because I want to be in control of my life. Never, ever do I want anyone to ever have the power over me to put me somewhere where I don't have food to eat, to put me somewhere where I don't know if it's safe to sleep, where I put myself and my children possibly in a place that is not so okay. I want to be in control of my life. I want to be able to choose on a Thursday afternoon to drive myself to the school and to go and pick my children up. I want to be there every Saturday and teach them little league sports because I can, and because I have the choice. I'm in control of my life."

Eureka! That was the breakthrough for him. That was his seven levels deep process. Once he understood that, he knew he was going to succeed in scaling up to the next level. The real reason that he was doing this was because he wanted control of his life, and he wanted to create choices for him and his family. Understand that when you go through this process, what I want for you is to find that deep, deep, deep understanding of why you want to embark on what it is that you really want to do.

Please do all seven levels, okay? You will feel the switch. And if you do have anyone with you where you are living right now, ask them to ask you the question so that you can reflect and answer, even if you don't answer them but you just write it down. I find it easier if someone else asks you the question, than if you ask yourself and try and answer, because it's difficult for us to go into our heart if we have to stay in the intellectual to ask ourselves the question. Does that make sense? So go ahead and try this process for yourself; a breakthrough is around the corner for you. I have prepared a "7 Levels Deep" worksheet for you, which you can download at www.connectedrainmaker.com.

Chapter 8

My Connector Action Map

Retracing the Map

> *"Relationships are all there is.
> Everything in the universe only exists
> because it is in relationship to everything else."*
> – Margaret J. Wheatley

Next, we will prepare to put your connector strategy into a planning document to take action. Just because it's planned, does not mean that it's not authentic. Do you see that?

Do you remember the Clarity Mapping Tool, where I used the example of the white river rafting in Colorado? I said to you that it was very important to get a laser-sharp focus of what direction you want to go to in your life, because that would dictate where, why, who and how you would engage people. If you reflect back, you will realise that the Clarity Mapping Tool was the first step to formulating your Connector Action Map. However, we built on that, and we went deeper and deeper in terms of your reflection, in terms of your understanding of self. This is not something that is common for every person to do. Truly, there are people in their 50s and 60s that I coach, in high-profile positions, who have never answered these questions for themselves.

For bonuses go to ...

It does not matter where you find yourself right now; the important thing is that you do it as quickly as you can. Just take messy, imperfect action.

We identified that there are five steps that we go through in order to develop a Connector Action Map. And we started step number one with the **origin and the history of relationships**, the reptilian brain and looking at some of the principles regarding relationships, like the importance of energy in relationships, followed by a look at step number two, **the connector mindset**. We then moved into step number three, **the connector strategy**. And we looked primarily at three components, the "who," the "what" and the "why."

So, we looked at the "big who," okay, and we then considered shifting our thinking and trying to understand more about defining our value when we connect with people through either caring or sharing/serving. I guided you to look at different currencies that you can develop in "general," "personal life focused," and "business life focused." And lastly, I shared with you the "big why exercise," called the "seven levels deep exercise." All of this is now going to form the foundation for step number four, which is about **researching and planning** towards step five, which is about creating a **Connector Action Map**.

The Navy Seals are trained in an approach called the Triple "A" Approach, where you ASSESS the situation, you ADAPT, and then you ACT. What you do is that you evaluate or assess what the need is that has to be dealt with, and then you adapt by getting the resources to do it; and then you execute or act in a way that's going to be successful to the mission. This is something similar to what we are going to do now. I want you to walk away with very simple yet profound concepts, which will absolutely not only magnify your ability to reach people, but also to connect with them, to get to know them and to truly enhance your life and business overall, when you look at the relationships around your business, and as a result magnify your impact and your feeling of being fulfilled in life. If you are in an organisation right now that can benefit by looking at its stakeholder relationship management and teaming, go to my website at www.leadercurrencybook.com to see how I can help you.

One can create different circles. Some can be inner circles. Some can be outer circles. There are relationships that will be transactional, and some relationships will be beyond transactional. Transactional means discontinuous. The ones beyond transactional means continuous recurring relationships. So you can think about these relationships in terms of value, the value you can give and the value you can receive. A relationship is steered by the 3 G's: GIVING, GETTING and GROWING. If we, however, want the third G, the growing part, as part of our relationships, it's sometimes about deliberate intent.

If you don't build rich relationships, and you don't reach out to those rich relationships in a planned effective way, and then serve them and be the kind of person that they want to hang around, then you will not achieve the results you are hoping to achieve—it will be mediocre.

The Poor Kid from Pittsburgh

"Never believe that a few caring people can't change the world. For, indeed, that's all who ever have."
– Margaret Mead

Keith Ferrazi is an American entrepreneur and recognised global thought leader in the relational and collaborative sciences, and he has been an inspiration to me, helping me realise that the spirit of Ubuntu is not only an African concept. I want to share his story with you. If you go way back, he was a poor kid from Pittsburgh, with a working dad and a cleaning lady mom, with education being his focus as a child. But more importantly, along the way, he was blessed with a few lessons from his father, who helped him understand that only through

For bonuses go to ...

other people will you be successful. And the criticality of reaching out to those people, with authenticity and generosity, is the same lesson that my father taught me.

He also learnt lessons from his mother. When he was doing research, he had a memory from childhood, where he remembered that his mother used to have a group of ladies that would come to their home, once a month, and so he called his mom and asked her about it. She immediately knew what he was referring to and said to him that they were the Card Club Girls, a group of ladies that met once a month for over 55 years. Phenomenal, isn't it? This group of ladies had been meeting without fail, without cancellation, for over 50 years. He asked his mom to tell him more about the group. How important was it? Why was it important? She said, "Well, when your dad was unemployed, that group of ladies would cook extra. And when your dad was out looking for work, they would bring a pot down with extra food. And I was able to put it on the stove and pretend to your father that we were able to stretch $1 so that we wouldn't have to eat welfare cheese."

In the United States, at the time, when your unemployment insurance ran out, and the government money ran out, they would give you cheese, government cheese, to basically sustain you. She went on to say, "But we never had to eat welfare cheese, because that group of ladies always cooked extra and brought it down to the house, so your father's pride would believe that even though we were very poor at the time, we were able to stretch $1 and put food on the table." She then went on to explain that when his aunt passed away a few days before, they thought about cancelling the card club, but they didn't cancel it. Instead, what they did is that they all came around his aunt's bed, they sat along the side of her bed, they played cards with her and they said goodbye. And subsequently, when his father passed away, those ladies came down and made sure that his mother got out of the house every single day for months, until she was ready to move on and get out of the house for herself. As he reflected on that story, a couple of realisations emerged for him.

He recognised that he didn't have that in his life. As a leader and as an entrepreneur running a company, he was not running a company where his team had that for each other. In that moment, that level of lifelong relationships became, for him, the kind of relationships that would set a North Star; it was the early germination of his definition of co-elevation, where a group of individuals were open and vulnerable to each other, being mutually and deeply generous to each other, and they were thinking about each other even when the other person wasn't around. This story that he shared was so inspirational to me at a significant level, because I realised that this notion of Ubuntu was not just an African concept, but successful entrepreneurs in the USA were also acknowledging the importance and impact of relationships, the real leadership currency.

Since then, Keith has come to understand that we are all different—some people are shy, and others have a big personality—but that you don't have to be like someone else; you have to be you. And the way in which you choose to be you has to create an environment around yourself that invites people in. But most of that is letting your guard down and being yourself. One of the most important things is to be purposeful in your relationship management, and to be purposeful doesn't mean fake. It just means to get it right. Fake means you're fake. If you're running around passing out business cards, you know that all you're doing is making contact, not relating, and we're talking about relating as the element of importance. And you may not even be connecting; you may just be annoying, or be one of those people that are experienced as a brownnoser, which you know we all feel uncomfortable with. The key is to be very purposeful and planned, because you don't have much time. Spend time with the most important people that are critical for advancing your mission.

For bonuses go to ...

It's so important to open people up to be authentic, real and connected as individuals. Keith says: "Find a way to care about each other, and find a way to help each other," which is similar to what I have told you in regard to being caring and sharing. So really, genuinely connect with people, and keep that relationship building. If you don't build rich relationships, and you don't reach out to those rich relationships in a planned, effective way, and then serve them and be the kind of person that they want to hang around, then you will not achieve the results you are hoping to achieve; it will be mediocre.

We will now take a closer look at how we go about planning to prosper.

Planning to Prosper

> *"I fear not the man who has practiced 10,000 kicks once, but I fear the man who has practiced one kick 10,000 times."*
> – Bruce Lee

The tool that we use to plan to prosper is the Connector Action Map. The first step of the Connector Action Map, is to identify your goal you want to move forward with. Be sure that it's a SMART goal, and then divide that into sub-goals. This is Strategy 101, which I am sure you already know; it's just a reminder. If you are not sure what a SMART goal is, you can download an explanation from my website, at www.connectedrainmaker.com.

Okay, so for step number two, this is about who to target. Think about the type of people that you would need to engage to make your project a success. This might be people like financiers, accountants, social media specialists and more specialised people in line with your specific topic. Then you start doing the research to see who the people are that you actually want to engage with, and you start understanding more about what is important to them, in order for you to start planning some suggested ways in which you can serve that person. If you knew one person had a sick child, for example, and did not know what to do to help them anymore, and you happened to know a medical specialist for this particular disease, you might offer to facilitate a meeting between them. Remember that we are in the planning phase now, so we can no longer be in the superficial; we need to now dig deeper. When we connect with people, we must be authentic. It's not just about what we want. It requires planning to see what it is that you have to do to be of service to that individual as well.

Once you have identified who some of the type of people will be that you want to engage and build a relationship with, what is important is that you track if a specific relationship is going to go into the quality or quantity column. So, at what level do you plan to build this relationship, because that will help you to see where you need to put more priority, more attention and more effort; so more energy, in order to bring those relationships up to the level that you would like them to be. I explained to you earlier that when we engage in relationships, it doesn't just happen by accident. You have to put the effort in, and you have to put the love in and be deliberate in your approach, if you want that to contribute to your life mission, or to be impactful to more people.

Very often within my relationship community, there could be someone that would like to meet someone else that I know. In this instance, I would typically call the other person, ask them permission to give their phone number to this individual, explain the context and then return back to the other person with a number, after I have permission to give it to him or her. Then I would tell them that the person is expecting the call. An alternative is that I may send an email, where I put both of them on the email, one in copy and one in the email itself, and then I write an email to say I thought that it would be a good idea for the two of them to connect, and that they're more than welcome to reach out to me if they would like to understand more before they respond to the person. So it's my relationship with each of them that

For bonuses go to ...

has allowed me to put them together through an email. You might want to extend your generosity in that way.

You need to make connection points, touch points. This can be different things; it can be a WhatsApp message, or it can be an email of a specific research article that might be interesting to that person. Don't make a nuisance of yourself; don't suddenly do it every day, but every now and then remember them, and just connect with them again. Also important is to keep it natural. Okay? What this is doing is that it's building your currency, showing your authenticity, the fact that you mean to build this for the longer term, and the fact that you want to create a trust-based relationship, which is first about giving. This is very important.

Taking Action

> *"I've missed more than 9000 shots in my career.*
> *I've lost almost 300 games. Twenty-six times,*
> *I've been trusted to take the game winning shot and missed.*
> *I've failed over and over and over again in my life.*
> *And that is why I succeed."*
> – Michael Jordan

As you take action, one of the steps that you might want to take is to first go and identify one or two names on the list that you've built as categories or types of people that you have chosen. You are now going to design your meeting strategy with that person. Based on your research, you will then decide what you can share or serve with; we always lead with what we can give. And then you will engage and identify some type of meeting time, and actually go ahead and have the meeting.

I want to remind you that what you are doing right now is something that only 5% or less of the world do; so of course, there will be a little bit of discomfort. The good news is that whatever you do, you cannot mess it up, right? Because if you are doing some preparation versus no preparation, you will always be in a stronger position than the average person. Does that make sense? So, if you were just doing nothing, that would be your worst case, because then you would be in a similar boat to everyone else; you would have to draw on your charm, or you would have to draw on just your natural talents, what we sometimes refer to as shooting from the hip, which is not ideal. The fact that you are actually going through this process of planning and researching in order to take action, means that you're already one step ahead. It's not about perfection, so don't think of this as a mathematical formula, where there's an exact answer. So therefore, I'm doing it right, or I'm doing it wrong. It's not like that.

Just go through the steps, and even if you don't have all the answers, you are starting to build a muscle. It's a little bit like the very first time you tried a new sport, or the very first time that you went to the gym and you did a new type of exercise. In the beginning, it's uncomfortable; you don't even know how to position yourself. Do any of you play golf? You have to put your arm like this, and move your legs apart and really be stretching the right way. It's complicated for the first few times, until you start getting used to it. And it's a similar thing that you're going through now.

Don't feel weird as you are doing it. Just be natural. Remember that this is not about you; this is about them. This is about them knowing that this is not only about what you are getting out of this conversation; it's also about you wanting to bring value to them as well. And it can be something as simple as making sure that they are having a good day so far. Think about if the roles were reversed, and you had a conversation with someone that cared about your best interest and wasn't only calling you to make a transaction to see what they can get. Go for it, and don't wait; set up your first meeting.

For bonuses go to ...

The advanced approach to this step is building towards teams or communities that co-create or create together in a synergistic way. It's the Ubuntu principle of togetherness, where a few different parties together can increase or elevate their impact with more resources, more knowledge, more impact and more service, than merely trying to do it on their own. So essentially, what it's saying is that if you are alone, versus if you are a team with the same mission, working together, the team will always achieve more and have a bigger impact than the individual alone. You can build this in different ways. One way is to connect with connectors—other people that value relationships and have many high-value relationships. Another way in which you can use your Connector Action Map process is to support yourself with the right people in your life, in terms of the skills that you need to learn. Coaches and mentors will fall into that category. At some point in your career, if you do this right, you will graduate from networks and move into teams or communities. Everyone works towards the same purpose, and therefore the purpose is reached much quicker.

Why a Coach?

> *"A coach or a guru is like a live road map.*
> *If you want to walk uncharted terrain,*
> *I think it is sensible to walk with a road map."*
> – Jaggi Vasudev

We don't always have to reinvent the wheel or learn through our own mistakes; we can observe and learn from those that have walked the path before us, and we can learn through their experiences. I believe that we should be lifelong learners. In fact, if you're looking for a coach right now, the first question you should ask is, "Who's your coach? Because if they don't have a coach, they're probably not going to be a good coach for you. Life is about evolving and learning. You also want a coach that has had failures in their life, so that they'll let you fail. They'll teach you and help you learn from your failure. A good coach

www.connectedrainmaker.com

doesn't keep you from failure, just like a good parent doesn't keep their children from falling down; it is a fallacy. They are just there to help you up and to help you learn lessons when you do fall down. But of course, that means that we first need to take a look at ourselves and be courageous and vulnerable enough to say, "What is it within me that I can adjust?"

You need a coach or a mentor to support you because, very often, it's hard. Even if you hold the mirror in front of you, it's hard to be able to see for yourself without the guidance of someone helping you to recognise that, to identify what that is. So it starts with you looking in the mirror. The first step in getting the right coach in your life is looking in the mirror. And honestly, looking at that person staring back and saying, "I'm ready to learn, I'm ready to be coached, I'm ready to do whatever this person that I've chosen shares with me to do. I'm ready." And most people say, "I just need a coach; I want a coach," instead of saying, "I'm ready." In India, there is a saying: "When the student is ready, the guru will appear." So say: "I'm ready." Being ready is the most important step. I could deliver the best coaching you're ever going to have in your life, but if you're not ready, it will amount to zero. It won't amount to anything; that relationship is over before it starts. Only when the student is ready, the guru (coach) can appear. If you want to learn more about how to be coached by me, please go to www.connectedrainmaker.com.

Know that a coach can't do the work for you; you have to do it yourself, but they can guide you to do the things that matter, to get the results you are aiming for. This goes back to fundamentals. Whenever you choose to accomplish something, make sure that it's worthy of you, because we all have the same amount of time. And make sure that your goal is going to be worthy of your efforts. When you work for this worthy goal, understand that you become what you think about, because thinking is a precursor to action. You have to ask yourself if this is right. Is it moral? Is it going to make me money? Is it going to be something my parents would be approving of, and that my society

For bonuses go to ...

would approve of? The question is, what goal are you trying to achieve?

In *The Strangest Secret*, Earl Nightingale refers to the following metaphor, and he says: *"The person who says to the wood burning stove, give me heat and then I will give you wood...well, he will be cold; it's cause and effect."* We must lead with giving. Before we become a getter, we must give of ourselves, our talent and our knowledge, and build a genuine relationship, without thinking about what you want from it. Often, when I coach business people, I will ask them what the first goal is that they would like to work on, and many say they want to make a lot of money. My response is to ask if they are clear on what they are going to do, to add value to the situation. Somebody will want to give you money for what you have to offer, if you are solving a need for them. You see, you need to lead with giving, and the getting will follow. In coaching, we talk about how, if you want to be competent in anything, you need to be competent in three domains:

- The first is the "I domain," which is self-management.
- The second is the "we domain," which is relationships and communication.
- The third is what everyone is looking for: the social, economic and livelihood, and all of that is received because you have done the first two.

The Power of Connectivity

> *"When you start to develop your powers of empathy and imagination, the whole world opens up to you."*
> – Susan Sarandon

I was very inspired and captivated by an interactive artist, Ivan, whom I came across thanks to TedX (you can go to my website, www.connectedrainmaker.com, to get the link if you want to watch it). He found a way to use his art in collaborative projects, bringing strangers together in unexpected ways. I would like to share his story with you to illustrate how he transformed 30,000 emails into handwritten letters.

As a child, Ivan was, as he described, lonely and kind of disconnected. He was the only Jewish kid in his school, and he got bullied for that. He didn't have a Christmas tree. He didn't know what the Simpsons were, and he wanted to know how people related, and how they created connections.

In 2011, Ivan got his dream job at one of the top ad agencies in the world, in Amsterdam. He moved from the US to Europe and was excited to meet new people and to travel Europe. Soon, he realised that he was spending most of his time in an office, and again he felt lonely and isolated, and was really feeling a bit annoyed with all the emails that were constantly filling up his inbox. He realised that email was his only connector method at the time, but the process felt disconnected to him, or at the very least, superficial. After 5 months at his dream job, he made a difficult decision and quit his job, without any other plan in place. All he knew was that he was passionate about connection, and he wanted to experience it in a more meaningful way than email. He decided to work with something unusual: handwritten letters, which some of us refer to as "snail mail."

About a week after he quit his job, he started this new project, leveraging hand-delivered mail to force himself to write more letters, and also to inspire more people to get acquainted with this lost art. About a week later, he had the inspiration for this project, which he called "Snail Mail," and he sent out an invitation to anyone in the world to send him an email and a recipient's physical address, and he would endeavour to handwrite it and then put it in the mail and send it anywhere in the world for free.

For the first few days, he got about five to ten letters per day, but then on the fourth day, it got a lot of press coverage. And on that fourth day, he got over 1000 letter requests, and he didn't have the time or resources to fulfil that. He put a note on a website that he had started for the project, asking if people would be willing to help out. Thankfully, support responses started rushing in. At that moment, the project turned into volunteer letter artists helping out, which in today's context is a crowdsource project.

One of the letters said: "Andy, while you're hard at work, I am at home making blueberry pancakes while naked." The letters really spanned all shapes, sizes and colours. They had letters sent all around the world, in different languages too. They had letters of acceptance from the Hogwarts School of Witchcraft and Wizardry, and they even had marriage proposals. The volunteers ranged from middle-class American moms, to even middle-school students in the Czech Republic, who got assigned it for their art class. And at the end of the day, the project existed for a period of six years. And during that time, the project had 2000 volunteers that sent out over 29,000 letters, and the volunteers paid for all of the postage.

What Ivan showed me through this beautiful practical example is that not only can we use the power of connectedness in any field to make an impact, but we can also use it in an increasingly divided and digital world, where human connection is more important than ever. These moments of connection are available to us all, although it also involves some degree of rejection; not everyone wants to participate. Still, at the end of the day, whatever it is that you would like to achieve, will happen with or through other people, because relationships are all there is. Ivan's work reminds us that it's more important than ever to cultivate simple yet profound moments of connection, which are always available to us. In the next chapter, we will explore the "magic sauce" that makes it all work. We will look at what to keep in mind when we build our connections.

Chapter 9

What to Keep in Mind When You Build It

What Is the Magic Sauce?

"Synergy is better than my way or your way. It's our way."
— Stephen Covey

Sometimes building relationship is intentional. You build it on purpose, for a specific intention. Sometimes relationships start unintentionally. You just happen to meet someone, and then it happens. Understand that relationships can be personal, and relationships can be professional. Sometimes it starts as a personal relationship, and it turns out to become a professional relationship. And sometimes it's a mix of both. Sometimes it starts professional, and then it ends up personal.

When we look at the broader definition of a relationship, it can be positive, and it can be negative (toxic). Take these dynamics into consideration when thinking of the concept of relationships as a broader definition. For the majority of the time, we will focus on the positive or value-added relationships, which are authentic and trusting, but we will also at times acknowledge the other side of the coin, and consider how to make the opportunity a value-added learning experience. There is no point in looking at the one side without acknowledging that there is another side; there are two sides of the coin.

For bonuses go to ...

Sometimes when we say "relationship," we tend to only see the positive, yet there is a negative side to relationship too. There are ones that will shrink you; ones that will make you lose yourself and sometimes lose others. Many of you reading this book might be in business, or planning to go into business, and it's important to know that people have lost businesses because of relationships, including myself. And people have created mega businesses because of relationships; again, I speak of first-hand experience.

Jack Ma, the founder of Alibaba, is a very good example of this. He was born in China and came from very humble beginnings. China was still amongst the underdeveloped countries at the time, but Jack was trying to work hard, and he had a vision. Jack Ma aspired to do something special with his life. He realised that if he wanted to create something that would impact his life, his community, his country and the world, he would have to grow his vision outside of himself, outside of his own thinking, outside of his country and even outside of his world. So what did he do? He started to learn English, because he understood that English was the business language of the world. There were people coming to China who spoke English, and he made sure he got closer to those English tourists, and he started to learn English. He tested his level every day with those people. He also used this opportunity to understand the world better through their eyes. He was trying to intentionally build relationship with the tourists, because there was a purpose in the relationship, to learn English and to get information about what was happening outside of what he knew. And he had coined two terms, which he uses today in business:

- Don't just stay with the known; try also to explore the unknown.
- Your relationship then should enable you to explore the known, but also to explore the unknown.

He had so much persistence, even though he had been continuously rejected earlier on in his life. After his schooling, Jack applied to university, and he failed the entrance exams three times before finally joining Hangzhou Normal University. He even applied and wrote to Harvard University ten times, and got rejected each time. Once he had received his bachelor's degree, Jack tried to apply for a job at many different companies, and continued to be rejected. In one of his interviews, he even referred to a time when KFC came to China, and they had 24 applicants that went to apply for jobs. Even at KFC, 23 people were accepted, and the 24th person was Jack Ma—rejected again. After finally coming to terms with all of his rejections and failures, Jack Ma visited the US in 1995, for a government undertaking project related to the building of highways. It was then that Jack Ma was first introduced to the internet and computers. He then searched "China," and not a single result popped out! He decided it was time for China and its people to get on the internet. Finally, after persuading seventeen of his friends to invest and join him in his new e-commerce start-up, Alibaba, the company began from his apartment. Relationships were the magic sauce, and the rest is history. Jack Ma is now officially one of the richest men in China. Alibaba and Jack Ma, although not household names out of China, are worth more than Facebook, and process more goods than eBay and Amazon combined. This is the beauty of relationship. Was it intentional? Was it unintentional? We don't know. But one thing we're sure about is that the friends agreed on sitting down together and building their relationships, to nurture them for a common dream, a common future. Having the shared vision, this is where the magic happened.

How Many Faces Do You See?

"Miracles happen every day; change your perception of what a miracle is, and you'll see them all around you."
– Jon Bon Jovi

Let me ask you, how many faces do you see?

For bonuses go to ...

If you want to see a copy of the real size picture, then go to my website, www.connectedrainmaker.com, to download the full-size, full-colour, print-ready version.

When I ask this to a group of people and ask them to shout out what they see, I often get varying responses; people will shout out 3, 4, 5, 6 and more faces, even though everyone is looking at the same picture. Why is this? We're all looking at the same picture. But it's all about perception. It does not matter what your answer is; you are right. It's based on your truth. And that's okay. Just know that there are multiple versions of the truth in one situation...take a moment to take that in.

What often happens is that when I initially ask people to look, they might see four, for example, and then they believe they have arrived at the right answer, until someone else sees 5, or 6, or 7 or even 8, and as someone lifts the barrier to the possibility of more faces, they realise there are more possibilities. They then research more. But sometimes they get to a point where they stop because most people see the same thing, and then they believe that they have reached the correct answer, the perfect answer—until the first breakthrough when someone sees a new answer again, and so it goes on. How many faces did you see? Can you see how this also happens in life?

Part of the challenge is, of course, our understanding of the instruction. You see, I deliberately asked how many faces you see; I did not clarify if I meant human faces or animal faces. Now take this scenario to a boardroom, or when we are speaking to other people. We often assume that we understand the same definition, but in this example, you might have counted all faces, or you might have self-selected that I meant only human faces. Can you see how you would automatically get a different answer depending on which approach you used?

What happens is that our definition for faces might be different. So for me, I might be including animals and people in my count of faces, while someone else might be thinking that a face must be attached to a human, so they would then not count the bird or the dog. One or the other could be right, or both could be right, but the problem is not about which one is right. The problem is that if we are not counting the same faces, we will be getting different results and not understanding why one person is getting one thing and another person is getting another thing. Do you see what I mean?

I see this very often with employees when sitting in a boardroom having a discussion about a challenge. No one really takes the time to check in on their understanding of the situation; they assume that they all see the scenario in the same way, instead of making sure that everyone is speaking about the same thing. One team might be speaking of "human faces." Another team might be speaking about "all the faces," including dogs and birds in the picture. And now they start arguing with each other because the one says the other one is ridiculous. But they don't realise that they're not speaking about the same thing.

In real life, I experienced this in the banking industry with one of my clients. One group, from the same bank, was from personal banking, and the other group was from corporate banking. Each area in the bank had their own organisational jargon that they used amongst

For bonuses go to ...

themselves. Acronyms would be thrown around wildly. The people were from the same bank, corporate banking and personal banking, and I put them in the same room, and we started having a discussion. Soon, they started using acronyms in the discussions, and the fight started happening. Then I said to them to stop using acronyms: "Even though you are in the same company, say the acronym in full, at least the first time you mention it; don't assume others know what you are saying, and let's see if we can get any further with your search for a solution." When they started explaining the acronym before they used it in conversation, they realized that in the same bank, in different departments, the acronym (the same word) meant different things to corporate banking and different things to personal banking. Can you believe it? They were fighting with each other, but they were not even speaking about the same thing. Where might you be experiencing this in your life?

I want you to remember that when you think about the models and the frameworks that we create for ourselves, the problem is not who's right or wrong. The problem is that when we are in a relationship, we have a conversation, and very often we assume that we see things the same way. Therefore, when we don't get to the same conclusion, we start arguing or fighting. This is in your personal life, but I see this happening often in business as well. We don't even realise that we're doing it. It can have such a big impact on you. As you start designing your relationship strategy, be aware of the fact that you sometimes have to reframe and challenge your mental models, linking this to the preparation in your connected mindset as you move into building your connector strategy. When you have well-designed models of reality, then that empowers you to feel good about yourself, and powerful in shifting the world to match the visions in your mind.

Richard Branson is an inspiring example of someone that challenges the current rules, and even ignores them; he makes his own rules and it makes others happy, and they adopt his way of doing things. And it has brought great success, great joy and great fulfilment for him and for others. I'm really encouraging you to think about what you want. Until you are clear about what you want, and what you want to contribute, there's no point in building the connector strategy, because you are going to bring the wrong people into your life; they're not going to necessarily buy into your vision if you're not clear on what that vision is.

Code of the Extraordinary Mind

> *"Epic things start with small, humble steps.*
> *Pay respect to your beginnings. And if you're just starting out,*
> *know that it's okay to be sucky. To be small. To be messy*
> *and chaotic. Just make sure to never stop dreaming."*
> *– Vishen Lakhiani*

Vishen Lakhiani shared this concept with me about "the code of the extraordinary mind." This is really something worthwhile to consider and think about as we move into building our connector strategy. So what is that about? Vishen came up with this concept that we have four levels that we move in, in order to become the best version of ourselves.

The first level is living in what he calls the **culturescape**. From his perspective, the culturescape is the world of relative truth, which is made up of human ideas, cultures, mythologies, beliefs and practices. So essentially, these are rules or expectations made up by other human beings, but they've been made up consistently from one generation to the next, to such an extent that we always believe, or we feel the pressure that we also need to achieve that. For example, many people feel the pressure that at a certain age, they need to be married; otherwise, it's too late for them. Or they feel that they have to have children at a certain age, because their biological clock is ticking. Or some people think that if they haven't made it financially by a certain age, they're done and they will never be able to make it.

Now all of those are relative truths. And the beauty of it is that you don't have to buy into them; you choose to buy into them because of generational programming.

The second level is the level of **awakening**, and it's the world we choose. It's no longer just doing what we think the world expects from us, but it is about choosing certain aspects that make sense to us in that world. For example, the culturescape might tell you, for example, that once you have finished school, the expectation is that you immediately need to go to university, or business school, and you need to get a qualification. And then you go out into the world. And if you don't do it like this, it's going to be difficult to be successful in your life. In the awakening phase—the world you choose—you will consciously say that you are someone that is more intellectual, and you want to follow that route, or you feel that your path is different and you're not going to follow that route. You might be entrepreneurial and say to yourself: "I already have a business idea that I want to start from the ground up, so I am just going to go and do it." One is not better or worse than the other. But it's a different thing if you choose it consciously, versus if you just take the next step because you think you have to do it, or because your parents said so. When you make your own decisions, you are moving into the awakening phase.

The next level is about **recoding** yourself. This is the world inside of you, which we have referred to already. This is when you start working on yourself and really gaining an understanding of what it is that you really want. Who are you really? How can you contribute to others? The Clarity Mapping Tool that we looked at earlier is exactly designed to help you get to the recoding phase. I want you to see that I have a very specific reason for introducing you to concepts in a specific order, and why I give you the activities that I do—it's tried, tested and has demonstrated results for me and for many of my students, clients and organisations. What you are doing is that you are starting to recode yourself, because you are starting to go into the world inside of you, and are trying to understand who you are. It's more about understanding yourself as an individual, and less about what other people are telling you that you are or should be.

The next level is the final level in this model, which is about **becoming extraordinary**. How do we become extraordinary? We not only change ourselves in the world inside of us, but we also bring this to the outside. We now start changing the world in a positive way, merely because of who we are as an individual. I'm not saying that all of you have to save endangered species of animals, or that you need to save the planet, from an environmental perspective. It's aspirational; if you want to do that, then that's wonderful. But some of you might think that this is not what you are envisaging for your life. All that you would like is to feel more fulfilled, or to be the best version of yourself, or to experience the world in a better way. That's a beautiful goal, in its simplicity. It doesn't always have to be this grand thing. The important part is that it really needs to resonate with you; it needs to make sense to you. Now that you have awareness, the idea is to first transcend the culturescape. So, not having to always do what you think is expected of you, like at a certain point getting married, then having children, then having to buy a house, then having a white picket fence, and maybe having a dog or a cat, and then becoming a mother or a father and getting a job. If that is something you really want, then that's different. But if it's not something that you want, but you feel the pressure from other people that you should be doing this, know that you are in the culturescape, and that's a very limited life.

Life can be much broader once you discover one simple fact, and that is that everything around you that you call life was made up by people. And these are people no smarter than you. So, there's no reason why you can't make up your own rules of what life should be. Once you learn that, you'll never be the same again. I'm sharing something slightly controversial, but I want to empower you so that you don't feel the weight of the pressures from the external world, and that you feel free to live the life that you want to live. That is how you're going

For bonuses go to ...

to make the contribution that you were born to make. Extraordinary minds are good at seeing the culturescape, and are able to selectively choose the rules and conditions to follow, versus those to question or ignore. Therefore, they tend to take the path less travelled, and innovate on the idea of what it means to be truly alive.

Is Relational Capital a Balance Sheet Entry?

"The best and most beautiful things in the world cannot be seen or even touched; they must be felt with the heart."
— Helen Keller

Relationships are central to almost everything in our lives. When we invest in our relationships, everything else is enriched in our lives. The first aspect of the relationship analogy is the relationship with yourself, as we have mentioned throughout this book. A very smart and interesting friend and colleague of mine, Professor Jon Foster-Pedley, a former airline captain, a senior executive for the European Space Industry, and a man that lived for a while in a Hindu Ashram, said to me: *"I'm a great believer in ordinary people. I think that being ordinary is more than enough. I think the ordinary human being with the ordinary brain, with the ordinary intellect, is actually a very great thing."* I didn't initially fully understand what he meant, and as we discussed it more, what he was saying to me became clearer. In effect, the term "ordinary people" refers to people that are just aspiring to live who they are. And that is sufficient, because we often look at someone else with admiration and think we need to be more of them, when in fact they should be doing them, and you should be doing you. You are the best version of yourself. And if you can authentically contribute that gift to the world, the most authentic version of yourself, that is a huge contribution to the world, possibly in the form of human capital, social capital, and the list could go on.

Beyond your relationship with yourself, then comes the relationship with others, the relationships with your immediate circle, and then the third level being your business relationships. Relationships are not about some sort of emotional urge to feel good; the true sense of relationships include the concept of collectivity, and are always underpinned with trust, authenticity and collaboration. Relationships in the business world are important. It's not the only important element, but it's a big and important aspect.

My first field of study was Natural Sciences, so I originally come from a scientific background, and I decided to do my MBA to learn about business, early on in my career. So entering my business studies, I was thinking with a scientific mind, and I raised my hand to ask what I thought was a valid question to the professor: "Professor, which part of the balance sheet actually represents the capital value of the human component in the business and the relational capital of the business? And then everyone burst out laughing. They thought I was trying to be funny, but truth be told, I was dead serious when I asked the question. I still have not received a satisfactory answer. For now, relational capital is a hidden asset. You'll never find it on the financial statement of a company. You'll find revenue, and you'll find expenses like chairs and cell phones and travel. But you won't find relational capital on a balance sheet. It is because accountants can't figure out how to account for it, or even measure the tangible value.

But a company that doesn't have relational capital has to spend a fortune in advertising to attract clients. A company that has amazing relational capital doesn't have to spend that much money. If we take Apple computers as an example, if you own a tablet made by Apple, you would never call it a tablet; you would call it an iPad. If someone says we're having a contest, and the prize is a tablet, everybody knows it's not an iPad, because people want Apple products. And if Tim Cook, the current CEO, announces they're coming out with a new product, he doesn't even have to say what it is; there'll be 10 million Apple lovers lining up with their credit card in their hand, saying to take their money—whatever it is, they want it, because people love Apple. Another example is Tesla. People who own a Tesla car don't say they have a car or an electric car; they proudly say that they have a Tesla. And you can go to General Motors or Ford and get an electric car for far cheaper, but they don't talk with pride about it. People feel they have a relationship with Tesla. They feel they have a relationship with Apple.

No matter if you are a man or a woman—it doesn't matter from which generation, and it doesn't matter from which country you are born—if you authentically implement the steps to be a strategic connector with a giving spirit, rather than engaging spirit, you cannot begin to imagine what can happen for you, and more importantly, you can impact and make a meaningful contribution along the journey. Relational capital has tangible, real value.

Social Media and Internet Have an Important Role to Play

"The first rule of any technology used in a business is that automation applied to an efficient operation will magnify the efficiency. The second is that automation applied to an inefficient operation will magnify the inefficiency."
– Bill Gates

The Earth is going through transformation. One of the things said a long time ago, by Sri Aurobindo, was about the concept of oneness, and he even predicted that we were going to develop technologies in the future, which were going to connect each one of us so that the distances between individuals from one continent to another continent would be narrowed. The internet and social media, although he did not know it at the time, is exactly that. Computation, internet and social media actually draw us together, connecting us. Through the online and virtual connectivity that is available to us today, we can build communities—communities that help each other with accountability, keeping each other accountable and asking the questions and getting the answers from each other. This virtual engagement has created opportunity for greater levels of transformation in more people, more than what most people could have achieved if they had served people in person, one on one only.

We could, however, argue that in the hands of a physician, a knife can save a life; while in the hands of a criminal who feels under pressure or afraid, and is going to attack someone with it, it can potentially take a life. But does that make the knife good or bad? Neither—it is the operator of the knife that will determine the outcome, right? The operator is the critical factor that determines how the object is going to be impacting. In the same way, the transformation that will occur, or the possibilities of transformation that can occur, through internet and social media, will again depend on the application of how it is used. It's just an additional resource that is offered to us, a powerful resource granted, but how we choose to use it is up to us. Wise people have said in the past that knowledge is useful, and technology is useful, but what is most important is the wisdom to use that knowledge and technology appropriately. Internet and social media can potentially play a role in expanding, not replacing, face-to-face engagement, and contributing heavily to relationship building.

Today, technology is an extraordinary opportunity to practice the principles of relationship building in a broader capacity. If somebody wants to get to know you, they now have the ability to get to know you without hunting you down in person—they can follow you on Twitter; they can be generous to you by re-tweeting; they can better understand who you are—because you're out there, and your profiles are updated. You can take a relationship, which started online, and move it offline if you want to, or you don't have to. There's nothing wrong with acquaintances. Not every relationship has to be what we call part of your "power of 5" group. You need those relationships. But

For bonuses go to ...

you also need the loose ties; the loose ties present opportunity. If somebody had a connection with you, even if it was just a loose connection, you might be willing to refer them to somebody else in your network. However, if you can't play to shared value, if it's just one-way traffic, it can become less valuable.

Social media is wildly more important than it's ever been. People who've never done anything except send emails or text, suddenly are wizards on Zoom, because that's how you have to communicate these days. It has forced many people to become better at the internet. If you've developed a rapport online, you might be willing to point them in the direction of some advice, or to somebody that could be of value. And that's fine; those acquaintances are fine. But it's almost like a funnel: You start with just those you follow because you want to learn from them. You then go to those you want to build some relationship with online. You then go to those who are offline relationships but still acquaintances. You then go all the way down to a real "power of 5" relationship. And if you just think of it as a funnel, it works beautifully. But you still have to apply the same basic principles in your planning process. Don't follow people randomly; think about what you want to achieve in your life, and follow the people that are in line with that. An example of using the funnel is that if you're in network marketing, and you want to find people to enroll—for example, if you're in sales, and you want to find prospects to sell your trinkets to—then instead of creating a deep relationship personally, by going to dinner with one person and making a big sale, you have a smaller, quality relationship with many more people in social media, where you can make an impact at a broader level, and therefore the value that comes back to you is greater, so you can make more money.

People are inherently capable of so much more than sharing, liking and tweeting; they just need to be empowered. It's easy to look at metrics and data and numbers as the only way to gauge success. I think when we do that, though, we kind of miss the mark and we're not actually allowing people to do as much as they're capable of doing.

As humans, we yearn to be seen, felt and connected with others, because we want to have a sense of belonging, and we want to feel understood. Virtually, it's easy to think about a stranger as someone that is separate from you, but what if you thought of the stranger as someone that you just haven't connected with yet? The magic in bringing our virtual connectivity options into the connector strategy, lies in being able to take the virtual elements, and social media, and reworking that into an intent of human connections.

The Lady with the Titanium Digital Rolodex

*"Skill is fine, and genius is splendid,
but the right contacts are more valuable than either."*
– Judy Robinett

When I spoke to Judy Robinett recently, the lady with the titanium digital Rolodex, and a woman whom I respect and regard very highly, she shared some insight with me about how important it is to engage the right relationships. She shared a part of her life story with me, and explained to me that when she didn't know a millionaire, she figured out very quickly that they think differently to the average person. She said that she had been raised to have a nine-to-five job. Finally, on a specific Sunday evening, she thought she was going to go nuts, and she felt nauseous about going to work the next day, to a 9-to-5 job, and she decided that she had to find a different way. She knew the way to do that was to meet people that thought differently than the "9-to-5 job people." It's intriguing because what happened was, as she managed to start hanging around them, she ended up adopting or learning from the millionaire mindset. They opened doors for her that she could have never opened. She looked at me and said, "Ezanne, it is really important that you always build your relationships up." She said, "Begin with the end in mind, what it is you need, and then figure out where the people are, where they hang out. Because you know, we're like chickens; we run around together."

For bonuses go to ...

She said that if you're looking for money, then you go to pitch events; you go to incubators, colleges and universities. What she found out with those groups was that members of these groups, at one time or another, were broke themselves, and all she needed was a little lifting up. Eighty-five per cent of people would love to help you, and the other 15% are the "bad actors," the dark triad. And one of my favourite quotes is by Oprah, who says: *"When someone shows you who they are, believe them the first time."* What I've learned is that the more success you get, the more prominent that behaviour becomes; it doesn't subdue. When you meet strangers, the first thing you look for is kindness. The second is a level of competency, and that takes a little bit longer to assess. But I always add generosity—just because someone can help you doesn't mean they will. And if they won't, they probably are narcissistic. It's better to kiss them goodbye. Find like-minded people that share your values.

There are 3 golden questions that you want to lead with when you meet people.

Number one is, "How can I help you?" And you'll get comfortable with that, as soon as you figure out that you have a lot to offer. The first thing is to have a kind ear; we all want to be heard, particularly now with the pandemic, and we'd all like to have good connections. People are very open to that. This is important to make sure people are generous and that they want to help.

The second question is, "What other ideas do you have for me?" Share your story, where you're at, what you're working on and what obstacles you have, and ask for advice.

And then the third question is, "Who else do you know that I should talk to?" This last one is just amazing. Often, you have no idea who the people that you know, know, and that's probably the biggest networking mistake that one sees—not using the people who are already in your network.

The good thing to realise is that there is no lack of resources out there; there are 7.4 billion people, 368 trillion in private wealth, no lack of money and no lack of information and ideas. They're all connected to people. Everything that you want to achieve, impact or connect— whatever it is you want to do—you can do it either with or through people. You cannot do it in any other way. Change will happen anyway, regardless if we do something or not. But if we want to do something in a meaningful way, some planning and maybe some deliberate action is required. That deliberate action often requires the assistance and support of other people, other relationships. Therefore, the three most powerful words in the English language, besides "*I love you,*" are "*please help me.*" It is thus very clear that to make our relational capital work for us, we must know how to work for it first. In the next chapter, we will explore the actions we need in order to get a good return on our relational capital (RORC).

Chapter 10

How to Get the Best Return on Relational Capital (RORC)

Be Vulnerable

> *"I spent a lot of years trying to outrun or outsmart vulnerability by making things certain and definite, black and white, good and bad. My inability to lean into the discomfort of vulnerability limited the fullness of those important experiences that are wrought with uncertainty: love, belonging, trust, joy, and creativity, to name a few."*
> – Brené Brown

There is a model that you can apply to get some of the critical aspects in place to maximise your chances on getting a good return on relational capital (RORC). This model is called the 4Rs model.

The first R refers to **reflection**. You must have that moment of imagination, of introspection; you must check yourself. Do you want to or need to do the mission you have selected, or not? The first person you must convince is yourself. It is absolutely the same in business, the same in relationship, the same in everything. The first person you must convince is yourself, the one you see in the mirror, so it's about reflection. The moment of introspection is first about

For bonuses go to ...

checking yourself. If you are still truly yourself, that's what you call authenticity. If you cannot even be truthful to yourself, I don't believe you will be truthful to others. This requires vulnerability.

I want to share a story with you that will highlight the power of vulnerability in relationships. The story is set in a country called Ghana, in West Africa. It was my very first time to visit Ghana, and I was going to work with a group of banking executives. I had done research and reading, but there was limited information available at the time, that would help me understand the business etiquette in Ghana better.

I was trying to prepare, largely because I'm respectful of the fact that if I go into an environment that I don't fully understand, or that I have not been to before, I need to be the one to inform myself so that I can demonstrate the required respect. In this instance, I flew to Ghana feeling somewhat unprepared; there wasn't much documented on the small nuances, the little things you need to know about African business in Ghana. It is not very well documented. Fortunately, I learned this concept of ego-free and vulnerability early on in my life.

I was with this group of banking executives, and I started the conversation by greeting them and expressing my intent of being there to serve. I also expressed my vulnerability, and that I was also coming to them with an intent to be respectful of their culture and their way of doing things, but that I might make mistakes unintentionally along the way, and that I would appreciate it if they could help me along the way.

In retrospect, I'm so grateful that I did that, because I was just halfway through an important conversation on the first day, and I had a pack of documents that I wanted to hand out to the group. I needed to distribute a copy of the document to each person in the room, and so for quicker execution, I divided the pack in half. With one hand, I gave the one half to an individual, and with the other hand, I gave the other half of the pack to another individual, and I asked if they could please

www.connectedrainmaker.com

take a copy and pass it on to other people in the room until everyone had a copy. A straight-forward task, right? Or so I thought.

To make a long story short, someone put up their hand and said to me: "Ezanne, you just cursed us; you have just insulted us gravely." "In fact," he said, "You used the F-word!!" My eyes were the size of saucers, and my eyebrows bent in at my brow; confusion was written all over my face. Carefully, I responded, "Hmm, in general, I'm not someone that uses profanity, and I don't really swear as a general rule." My first thought was that maybe my accent, maybe my pronunciation, wasn't that clear. So I said, "I'm not sure I really used the F-word; however, maybe my pronunciation made you think I used it. I am very sorry for that." The people in the group could see that I was struggling a little bit, not knowing how to respond to this comment. And then one elder compassionately put me out of my misery. She started laughing, and like a choir, so did the rest of the room. She said, "No, Nomvula, you didn't physically use the words; you implied the F-word by what you did!" She went on to explain to me that in Ghana—and subsequently, I've learned that this is not unique to only Ghana but is true in the Muslim religion and in some other context too—it is extremely rude to hand something to another person with the left hand. And by virtue of me taking two stacks of paper, handing them out with my left hand, and passing them to someone else, what I was really doing was something very disrespectful.

The critical part of the story that I hope you are following is that had I not been vulnerable at the offset of our meeting, I can tell you that with this unconscious disrespectful demonstration of mine, that the people would have completely disengaged, and the real message I was there to deliver would not have been received. Since I had started the conversation with vulnerability, it allowed for us to have full engagement and full transparency; there were no masks, and we were able to connect. Although they were very playful in the way that they communicated the message to me, I had the opportunity to learn and

For bonuses go to ...

to grow, and it gave us an opportunity to build a richer and deeper connected relationship. At the end of my workshop with the Ghanaian delegation, in their hospitable warm way, they arranged a field trip for us to go and explore special sights in Ghana together. They made me feel like I had become part of their community. The experience was unforgettable.

Be Ready

> *"Success is where preparation and opportunity meet."*
> — Bobby Unser

The second R in our 4Rs model is **readiness**—you reflect to get ready. Why do you want that readiness? It's all about the next R, which is **relevance**. The ones who are ready will have a higher probability of relevance. And believe me, relevance is going to influence your existence. When your relevancy is gone, your existence is gone. An example of that is Nokia or Blackberry. The only way to sustain existence is to sustain relevance.

Never go to a place without first doing deep research about that place; this is about readiness. You need to understand certain things about the market, about the place, the ways of doing things, what kind of mindset and biases and habits the people have, how to create relationships there, and how to sustain the relationships. Why? If I want to create an impact in that environment, I need to know where I can get my first local partner. Ask questions like: "What services do they have? What is it they're trying to achieve? What are their networks and connections?" You need to get all the information.

You start talking to people. Locate and talk to as many people as you can; find out what they need. The most important thing is to start by listening, which to me is the essence of it all. Close to the relationship, the relationship is about listening. Listen to as many stories as possible, until you can understand what the place is all about, what people are talking about, what's important to the people, what they need and what it is that excites them. To do that, you would have to spend time and to listen. Identify the critical things for them in their daily life, and then figure out a way to deliver that to them, and structure a business model around it. When one leads with a need to serve, then the rest will follow. If you lead with an open heart and you want to serve, the rest will come, and it will follow, as long as you are serving based on what people need, and not based on what you *think* they need. There's a very significant difference. So do the research first; do not jump in blindly.

There are a couple of things we need to understand, and one of them is the construct of shared value. To create shared value, everyone in the value chain has an intrinsic commitment to do something to contribute. When we bring greed into that equation, we destroy that opportunity, and you don't get the flywheel effect; you don't get momentum like when a whole bunch of people are making money. There are a lot of people that are influenced through a process like this, and the more you have, the more opportunity comes through. Not everyone's going to be thinking like that, but it's those that do, that can share with likeminded people around them (the power of 5); you kind of create a movement. And when you create a movement, you can do that.

A friend of mine, Brett Will, has an entrepreneurial flair and a big heart, and he shared the following story with me about what he and a fellow board member of his came up with during the COVID lockdown in South Africa. He said to me that he started by really trying to understand what the key issue about the problem was. Essentially, in the context he was looking at, parents were having to do home teaching for their children, and they were still trying to work while having to teach their children. What Brett tried to understand was what the intrinsic thing was that needed to be sorted out. What's the pain point that you want to go away with? What they decided was

For bonuses go to ...

that it was not just about schooling the children, but there was also a money issue. They spoke and they listened, and then they heard. Then they developed an online school, where you get home tuition but you can also pay according to your pocket. If you wanted the best math teacher, you paid a bit higher of a fee; but if your kid was really good at maths and you just needed someone that would challenge them, you could pay a different fee. In its first month, the business made a million.

The essence here is that the focus was on the community and its need and its shared value. And all those teachers who now weren't getting paid during COVID for extramural activities, or extra lessons, were making double their previous salary committed in that equation. So, when we look at turning around communities, it's not about what we can get; it's about what needs to be done to create a turnaround for the community. Approach the situation with an attitude of *"we didn't come here to do things to you; we came to do things with you."* Shared value is massive; share the pot of wealth. There's enough here for all of us. And it's not difficult to do when you create a movement. It makes me think of something I learnt from Tony Robbins. He said that if you have an attitude that **life happens for you**, and not that life happens to you, you will start seeing the opportunities, and you will also start working collaboratively.

Be Relevant

> *"Existence is no more than the precarious attainment of r elevance in an intensely mobile flux of past, present, and future."*
> – Susan Sontag

We need to make sure that we are relevant to the environment that we are in, too, as mentioned before. In order to be relevant, you need to ask, "How can I serve here? What is it that I can contribute to this environment, industry, place, market, community?" Before you can understand what is needed, you have to understand the context that you are operating in, and that is why we first looked at the "readiness." You need that information to make an impact. You only make an impact when you are offering people things that they need or are aspiring to. To establish what it is that you can start with, you need to establish what it is that's missing, that you can provide. As you consider your relevance, you want to consider what services already exist, what services people need and what it is that is missing here that people are yearning to have, which you may be able to offer based on your own authentic self and your strengths. You understand firstly how you can serve them, and then find out where the gaps are and what is going on in terms of the environment, and then create your product or service that addresses their need, and make sure that you do the best you can to deliver to the best of your ability, because that is going to give you prosperity. It is also going to ensure that you have customers for your business.

Raymond Aaron shared a story with me that I would like to share with you. He heard that there was a contest to choose the 12 most powerful salespeople in North America, and he decided to enter the competition. And he won. He was elected as one of the 12 most powerful salespeople in North America; this was about 20 years ago. He got to attend a course with those 12 people. And the instructors put them into pairs and said that the person on the left is person A, and the person on the right is person B. He instructed them to sell something to each other, and it could be at any price.

So Raymond (Mr. A) said to Mr. B, "Okay, I'm going to sell you a fleet of 100 Rolls Royce cars that never need any gas. And they all have a chauffeur that never sleeps, and they are at your beck and call at any time of the day. And it costs $1. Mr. B responded and said, "Okay, I'll buy that." And then Mr. B did the same thing with Mr. A, and Mr. A bought what was proposed. When the activity was over, the instructor asked them to put up their hand if they were successful at selling something, and they all put up their hands. Then the instructor said

For bonuses go to ...

to put up their hand if they had asked the other person what they wanted. None of them had done this. Raymond said to me, "Ezanne, we were so egotistical, including me, that we just thought of ourselves. 'Oh, I have a wonderful product, and I don't care if you want it. The price is so low, you will say yes anyway.'"

This story highlights the "relevance" part of the 4Rs model. Ignore anything about your needs as a starting point. Find out what the people, the community that you are engaging with, needs. And at any point in time, there's always something that many people need. An example is when Moderna was on the verge of being approved for its Coronavirus vaccine, and people wanted to know what the side effects were. If I sold a document for $10, or $1, about the real side effects of the vaccine, maybe a million people would have bought it. If I wrote an article on what the real truth of the Coronavirus was, and about what they're not telling you, lots of people would buy that.

Most people today sell what they want to sell. They miss the point. You need to provide what people would like or need. If you're a plumber and you have a plumber's qualification, and you like being a plumber, you go out and sell plumbing. If nobody needs a plumber, or if there are too many plumbers in your area, you might say to hell with that: "I'm a plumber; I'll just earn less money." Why not, instead of thinking of what you can do yourself, think of what they want. You could make more money than you could ever imagine, because you are bringing real value in line with what people need. If we are service oriented, and I don't mean the fashionable sense of how people use it loosely, but authentically wanting to serve the needs of another, it will just automatically come back to you. What's needed today is the creativity and the initiative to do what is needed, not what you want to do, and this is all about relevance.

Be Open to Listening

> *"I remind myself every morning:*
> *Nothing I say this day will teach me anything.*
> *So if I'm going to learn, I must do it by listening."*
> — Larry King

The fourth R in the 4Rs model is your **relationship**. Once you have taken the time to reflect, to do the research towards readiness, and you have identified a service of product that is relevant to the people you want to serve, you have to follow through with the fourth R, almost in tandem with the other processes, which is relationships.

You make friends, and you build the relationship. You build some special relationships, based on quality, and you need to reach a number of people, so quantity is also important. Based on the information you collected, you would then develop a plan, and you then have to put the plan out there. Today, the best way to get your message out is though social media; it is about excitement, and it is about creating a buzz around what you do. People should sit up and say, "Wow, we like that." You cannot do that if you don't understand what the people need and what excites them. Often, we miss that point. It is about finding what it is, and then honing in on that, and then covering as much as you can.

It's about building it now for the long-term return. It would be about listening, about understanding, making friends, building the relationships and then marketing what you've decided is right, to the people in a bigger way, and creating excitement. Most importantly, we must understand that we do business not only for profit; it is also about shared value. It's also to make a difference in people's lives. Now, that difference could be to give them a better quality product. It could be to give them a better price. It could be to give them accessibility to some things they don't have access to. In our minds, whenever we plan business, this is an aspect that should be there. Consider how what we are doing will make a difference to our customers lives or to the people that we are going to serve, because that should be our purpose; it cannot be purely for profit.

In Africa, where I come from, people understand that the true value and the true returns lies in relationships, and a critical part to building strong relationships is most certainly listening to those around you. My father shared many lessons with me that he learnt from his friend, the Zulu chief, about leadership, and one critical skill that any good chief has, is the ability to listen.

At times my father would go to tribal meetings, better known to us as an "Indaba" (Zulu word for meeting), with the elders. There were so many things that my father drew from these experiences, but some of the most noteworthy would probably be, they would always sit in a circle during their meetings, which meant that everyone could see each other and make eye contact, and the chief was always the last to speak. This is phenomenal, the top leader would speak last, so not only was it about listening, but Ancient African Wisdom had taught the tribal leaders that they need to learn to be the last to speak. You might ask, why would this be? In boardrooms today we see the complete opposite. Even people who consider themselves good leaders who may actually be decent leaders will walk into a room and say, here's the problem. Here's what I think, but I'm interested in your opinion. Let's go around the room. The problem with this approach is, that it's too late, you have already influenced the responses. The skill to hold your opinions to yourself until everyone has spoken does two things:

Firstly, it gives everybody else the feeling that they have been heard and it gives everyone else the ability to feel that they have contributed.

And secondly, you get the benefit of hearing what everybody else is thinking, before you share your opinion.

The skill is really to keep your opinions to yourself. Don't nod when you agree or disagree with someone, just be still and absorb it all. The only response you want to offer is an occasional question to ask for clarity in your understanding of their opinion. It is critical not only to hear what they are saying, but also to understand the context that is informing their thinking. Once everyone has contributed what they would like to share, finally at the end it will be your turn. In African leadership tradition, this is a given, but the way in which we have been taught in Western Society, makes this approach much harder to follow. If you get this right, it is also how, in time, you will receive loyalty and build a successful business. It has to start with the relationship, and with listening.

In Africa, we have had too many businesses that care nothing for the continent, or for the people of the continent, that have never listened to the people, and that have never built relationships. And at the end of the day, we can no longer do that. We need to listen to people, all people across the world. We need to make them part of what we do, and we will be successful. An old African proverb says: "*If you want to go fast, go alone; if you want to go far, go with others.*" Put in a slightly different way, when I spoke to Derek De Beer, Johnny Clegg's master drummer, a while ago, he so beautifully explained his view of connections: "*We are all angels with only one wing; we can only fly when we embrace one another.*"

Identify Your Dream Team

> "*In the moment of crisis, the wise build bridges and the foolish build dams.*"
> – Nigerian proverb

Who do you have with you to make all of it happen? Who will give you the time to reflect and be willing to reflect with you? Who will be willing to give you the space to build your readiness, and support you

For bonuses go to ...

in that journey to get ready, and be with you to sustain relevance, and challenge you to stay curious and be courageous to explore the unknown? These are the **3Cs: challenge, curiosity, courage**. If you really want to be successful, design a solution that impacts millions of people. And the quickest way to impact millions of people, is by having coaches and mentors in your life that can guide you through the steps. If you would like to know more about how I can help you gain clarity on what you want in life, or if you want help to create your leadership currency, please go to www.leadercurrencybook.com to learn more about these programmes and other ways that we can work together. When you start with the intent of building a business or wanting to achieve something through and with relationships, another thing that you must do—and it takes incredible courage and incredible confidence about who you are as a human being to do this—is to be unbelievably candid, honest and authentic with people around you.

Whoever came up with the phrase, *"fake it till you make it,"* needs to be just put on a desert island somewhere. "Fake it till you make it" is the worst advice that anyone will ever give you in your lifetime. Are you not sick and tired of the fakeness that comes your way? Then why would you ever want to consider making that part of your identity? Undoubtedly, you will be found out that you're faking it. Undoubtedly, people do not want to follow "fake"; they want to follow "real." They don't care if you're the most talented, but they do care if you are the most authentic and the most approachable. They don't care if you are the wealthiest, and they don't care if you are the smartest—they care that you're the most genuine.

What I can tell you is that if you are starting from scratch, whatever it is that you are about to do, do it with honesty, with character, with genuineness and with vulnerability. It takes no confidence and courage to fake it. But it takes incredible courage to be vulnerable. As humans, we are drawn to vulnerability and authenticity.

We want "real"; we want to commune with real people that have real struggles and have real lives. So consequently, if I were to start today, the first thing I would do is have a really crystal-clear "why" it is that I'm doing what I'm doing, and a really crystal-clear "willingness and openness for other people to help me." I would not do it alone. I would not even attempt to do it alone. But based on the clarity of my "why" and my "what," then I would look for the "who." It's the "who," not the "how," that matters. Who can help me? Who can join this dream team to make this a reality?

Many times, we get tripped up and swallowed up and smothered with the "how." "How" would I get to a million people? "How" would I get to a million dollars? In reality, it's the "who" that you should be thinking of. Even if I can't draw from past relationships, I would still identify the "who." "Who" would my dream team be, to reach a million people and generate a million dollars? And even if I don't know them, if my "why" is clear enough, and my "what" is tangible enough, I can absolutely bring them on board to my dream team. And collectively, we will get to that million dollars, and impact a million people. This has been done so many times, with a team but not alone. The only reason I can share this with you is because I got it wrong a lot of times before I realised the full picture. I want to be clear with you that this hasn't always been the way I thought, and that I made a lot of mistakes to get to this point, and that I've learned from those mistakes. And that's why I have the view that I have. I will never go down the path of a mission or a message or a passion, without a dream team. And that dream team doesn't even have to be paid; it can just be people who share in that dream and vision. But I will not embark on any journey that I have to embark on alone. If it is something I have to embark on alone, then I need to do some serious self-reflection, and make sure that this is actually something worth pursuing, because if I can't convince some other people that it's the right thing to do, it may not be the right thing to do. Sometimes we have to step back and say, "Wait a minute; if nobody is on my train, if nobody's getting on the bus with me, maybe this is not the right bus to be on." And you know, that's hard to do sometimes.

Cast a Big Shadow on Departure

*"I will greet this day with love in my heart.
For this is the greatest secret of success in all ventures.
Muscles can split a shield and even destroy life itself,
but only the unseen power of love can open the hearts of man."*
— Og Mandino

There is this beautiful concept in Africa, a Sesotho concept called "SERITI," which when directly translated means integrity. Philosophically, it is also the word for the shadow or aura that people cast as they go through life, a shadow that grows when you do good, and is diminished when you do bad. In essence, your *seriti* becomes your reputation and, ultimately, your legacy. The *seriti* is the metaphysical shadow that each of us possesses as human beings.

There is a physical shadow, but there is also a metaphysical shadow. In Zulu, there is a clear distinction made between the two shadows that you cast, the *"umthunzi"* which is your physical shadow, and *"isithunzi,"* which is your spiritual or metaphysical shadow. The best word I could relate this to in English is probably your aura or a presence. What is interesting about this concept is that only the things that are real, that are important, cast the shadow; it's not the cars we drive, the houses we live in, our bank balance or the degrees that we have. It's the relationships that we have cared for; it's the people that will come to celebrate our shadows at our passing, and the people that will tell stories of the significant way in which our shadows overlapped. We become the product of many relationships that we have had in our lifetimes.

With this in mind, the last component that will determine your return on relational capital, the value of your real leadership currency, is the size of your shadow. Think very carefully about the legacy that you want to leave, and be deliberate in living that legacy fully. The greater your legacy, the greater your impact on this world; the more people's lives you have touched, the more you will receive in return.

My wish is that in sharing this journey together, you will think back on this as a Kairos moment, because that means that you could relive the moment of insight, growth and development many years down the line. My wish for you is that you will express and grow a shadow that will be worthy of your life, be worthy of your contribution and be worthy of your legacy.

As we depart from this learning and growing journey that we have shared, I want to leave you with a lovely departure greeting. The greeting on departure is as equal and as important as the greeting on arrival. The greeting on arrival opens the doors to the conversation, and develops relationships. It's the greeting on departure that keeps the doors open. So I would like to keep our sacred door to our sacred connection open, with the following beautiful Zulu greeting on departure, which is, "*Abake a bonana bayo pinde a bonana phuti,*" which means, "Those of us that have seen each other, will surely see each other again." It means we have crossed paths and, just because we've done that, we will cross paths again in the future. I look forward to when our paths cross again.